WHITE SOX

2005 WORLD SERIES CHAMPIONS

SP
SPORTS
PUBLISHING
L.L.C.

www.SportsPublishingLLC.com

CHICAGO SUN-TIMES

PUBLISHER: John Cruickshank
EDITOR IN CHIEF: John Barron
MANAGING EDITOR: Don Hayner
SPORTS EDITOR: Stu Courtney
LIBRARY DIRECTOR: Deborah Douglas
PHOTOGRAPHY DIRECTOR: Nancy Stuenkel
DESIGN DIRECTOR: Eric White
VP MARKETING: Jaclene Tetzlaff

www.SportsPublishingLLC.com

PUBLISHERS: Peter L. Bannon and Joseph J. Bannon Sr.
SENIOR MANAGING EDITOR: Susan M. Moyer
ACQUISITIONS EDITOR: Joseph J. Bannon Jr.
COORDINATING EDITOR: Noah Adams Amstadter
DEVELOPMENTAL EDITOR: Travis W. Moran
ART DIRECTOR: K. Jeffrey Higgerson
BOOK DESIGN: Dustin J. Hubbart
DUST JACKET DESIGN: Joseph T. Brumleve
BOOK LAYOUT: Dustin J. Hubbart and Kathryn R. Holleman
IMAGING: Kenneth J. O'Brien and Heidi Norsen
PHOTO EDITOR: Erin Linden-Levy

Front cover photo by Tom Cruze/Sun-Times
Back cover photo by Jon Sall/Sun-Times

ISBN: 1-59670-102-1 (softcover edition)
1-59670-139-0 (hardcover edition)

Printed in the United States

Sports Publishing L.L.C.
804 North Neil Street
Champaign, IL 61820

Phone: 1-877-424-2665
Fax: 217-363-2073
www.SportsPublishingLLC.com

CONTENTS

EDITOR'S NOTE

Thank God, we don't have to hear them anymore. They were the two most frequently heard phrases in Chicago in the fall of 2005.

"Not since 1917 ..."

"Not since 1959 ..."

Those dates were, of course, the last times the Chicago White Sox had won/been in the World Series.

Now, to paraphrase White Sox TV announcer Ken Harrelson: *"They Gone!"*

The 2005 White Sox have brought glory on themselves, joy to a city and massive catharsis to the Windy City's previously bedeviled baseball fans. The *Chicago Sun-Times* congratulates the team and its entire staff for proving that big things can come from "small ball." The *Sun-Times* and Suntimes.com had a ball covering the team from spring training to the last sip of champagne. We're very pleased to present this book, which captures the outstanding coverage of our writers, photographers, and editors.

Save it, savor it and call upon it regularly to help relive our most exciting baseball season since ... (well, that's your call).

John Barron
Editor in Chief

A QUICK 1 AND DONE

WHITE SOX 1, INDIANS 0
APRIL 4, 2005
U.S. CELLULAR FIELD

The only blemish in a classic season opener was the way things were decided, not that anybody on the White Sox' side was complaining. Mark Buehrle and the Cleveland Indians' Jake Westbrook squared off in a game that was more like speed chess in the park, with the Sox squeezing out a 1-0 victory before 38,141, thanks to an error by Indians shortstop Jhonny Peralta.

In a 1-hour, 51-minute step on the accelerator, Buehrle's two-hit, eight-inning performance topped Westbrook's four-hit, eight-inning offering when Aaron Rowand's seventh-inning bouncer on a drawn-in infield caromed off Peralta's body, allowing Paul Konerko to score the lone run. Peralta replaced longtime Indians stalwart Omar Vizquel, who nearly signed with the Sox this offseason before joining the San Francisco Giants. Buehrle made his fourth-straight Opening Day start despite having only one spring training outing to get over a freak foot injury that team doctors called a stress reaction.

	1	2	3	4	5	6	7	8	9	R	H	E
Indians	0	0	0	0	0	0	0	0	0	0	2	1
White Sox	0	0	0	0	0	0	1	0	X	1	4	0

Indians	AB	R	H	RBI	BB	SO
Crisp, CF	4	0	1	0	0	1
Belliard, 2B	3	0	0	0	0	0
Hafner, DH	2	0	0	0	1	1
Martinez, C	3	0	1	0	0	0
Boone, 3B	3	0	0	0	0	0
Blake, RF	3	0	0	0	0	0
Broussard, 1B	3	0	0	0	0	1
Hernandez, LF	2	0	0	0	0	1
a-Cora, PH	1	0	0	0	0	1
Peralta, SS	2	0	0	0	0	1
b-Sizemore, PH	1	0	0	0	0	0
Totals	27	0	2	0	1	6

a-Struck out for Hernandez in the 9th. b-Flied out for Peralta in the 9th.

E: Peralta.

Indians	IP	H	R	ER	BB	SO
Westbrook (L)	8.0	4	1	1	1	3
Totals	8.0	4	1	1	1	3

White Sox	AB	R	H	RBI	BB	SO
Podsednik, LF	3	0	0	0	1	1
Iguchi, 2B	4	0	0	0	0	1
Everett, DH	3	0	0	0	0	1
Konerko, 1B	3	1	2	0	0	0
Gload, 1B	0	0	0	0	0	0
Dye, RF	3	0	1	0	0	0
Rowand, CF	3	0	0	1	0	0
Pierzynski, C	3	0	1	0	0	0
Crede, 3B	3	0	0	0	0	0
Uribe, SS	3	0	0	0	0	0
Totals	28	1	4	1	1	3

2B: Konerko; SB: Rowand.

White Sox	IP	H	R	ER	BB	SO
Buehrle (W)	8.0	2	0	0	1	5
Takatsu (S)	1.0	0	0	0	0	1
Totals	9.0	2	0	0	1	6

T: 1:51; Att: 38,141.

Starting pitcher Mark Buehrle goes to work in the first inning on Opening Day at U.S. Cellular Field. Photo by Al Podgorski/Sun-Times

White Sox manager Ozzie Guillen greets designated hitter Carl Everett as the starting lineups are announced on Opening Day.
Photo by Al Podgorski/Sun-Times

"You have to tip your cap to Buehrle," said Konerko, who was in position to score the game-winner after doubling to lead off the seventh and going to third on a fly ball by Jermaine Dye. "Those guys threw well today; our guy threw a little bit better. The guy Buehrle is unbelievable. I know his foot is bothering him, probably, but what can you say? Whatever the game is that day, it seems like he pitches to the game. If it was a seven-run game, he gives up runs when he knows he can do it. If it's a 1-0 game like it was, he just bears down. You can't put your finger on it. He's good."

Buehrle was perfect through four innings when Victor Martinez led off the fifth with a single up the middle through Buehrle's legs. But Martinez was erased one batter later on a double-play grounder by Aaron Boone. The Indians' only other hit was a single by Coco Crisp to lead off the seventh.

Shingo Takatsu pitched a perfect ninth for the save as the Indians sent only 28 batters to the plate, one over the minimum. Ross Gload, a defensive replacement for Konerko at first, made a diving stop on a Crisp grounder to make the final out.

The outing was similar to one Buehrle had last season against the Indians at Jacobs Field in which he pitched a two-hitter while facing the minimum 27 batters. And while that game came to mind Monday, Buehrle ignored thoughts about perfection.

"It kind of went through my head, especially when the guy got the hit and then the double play," Buehrle said. But it's just a long game. Once I get into the ninth inning, if I have something like that a perfect game, then I'll start to think about it."

There were signs Buehrle had the potential to be so dominating. He retired the first 12 batters he faced in a Cactus League game against the San

Diego Padres on March 8, and he pitched six perfect innings against the Kansas City Royals on March 19, the day before he injured his foot shagging fly balls.

"That's what we expect from him," manager Ozzie Guillen said. "I'm so happy he was healthy just to come out and perform. As long as he's healthy, that's what we're going to see from him. He threw a tremendous game."

Along with the two hits, Buehrle (1-0) gave up a walk and struck out five. Westbrook (0-1) walked one and struck out three.

"That's as good as I've ever seen him," said Indians manager Eric Wedge, somehow able to differentiate from Buehrle's outing last season. "Jake was outstanding. He was just like Buehrle. He was making his pitches and working corner to corner. The Sox just squeezed one run out, and that's all it took."

—Written by Doug Padilla

Paul Konerko leads off the seventh inning with a double off Indians Jake Westbrook. Konerko eventually scored the winning run when shortstop Jhonny Peralta couldn't handle Aaron Rowand's infield hit. Photo by Al Podgorski/Sun-Times

PODSEDNIK IGUCHI

OF, 2B

Podsednik, Iguchi Let Teamwork Speak

By Mike Mulligan

The lumber has been in a season-long slumber, but the top of the White Sox' batting order has exceeded all expectations. The Sox haven't had to wait for Scott Podsednik and Tadahito Iguchi.

"All in all, I think we've been a pretty good 1-2 tandem," Podsednik said of a teammate he has yet to have a conversation with. "He puts the ball in play, puts the bat on the ball, gets me over and gets me in. If it's not broke, I'm not going to try and fix it."

Like Podsednik, Iguchi is new to the Sox and arrived late to the major-league party.

Podsednik, 29, struggled in the minor leagues waiting for his break with Milwaukee, while Iguchi, 30, was a four-time All-Star in Japan.

"Right now, I am not satisfied with my batting at all," Iguchi said through his translator. "I think I can hit for a higher average, but at the same time if Pod gets on first base, it is my job to move him, and if that is going to help the team win, I am willing to do that. If it is not going to help the team win, I might try to do something else. But right now, it is working."

Does batting behind Podsednik hinder or help Iguchi? Given the leadoff man's speed and ability to wreak havoc on the basepaths, pitchers can get distracted. Catchers might call for more fastballs to improve their chances of getting the ball quickly to second base. But at the same time, Iguchi has to

lay off pitches, and that sometimes will put him behind in the count. And when Podsednik gets on second, Iguchi has to hit behind him and push everything to right to advance the runner.

"It is a benefit to have guys on base, period," Podsednik said. "I don't know what Iguchi is thinking. We haven't really communicated about running and hitting in certain situations just because of the language barrier. But for the most part, he's up there hacking. When he sees a good pitch, he's swinging. He's done a good job of putting the ball in play and getting me over in certain situations.

"I don't know if me being on base necessarily gets him more fastballs, but I do know the tempo of the pitcher changes. He comes over, and he's thinking about me a little more than he's thinking about the hitter at times, and I think that is to our advantage."

Los Angeles Angels manager Mike Scioscia, a former catcher, said having a speedy runner on base is an advantage if teams forget to deal with the man at the plate.

"Most pitchers aren't as comfortable out of the stretch, especially if they have to alter their delivery a little bit to be quicker to the plate," Scioscia said. "They won't put as much on the ball, so it is definitely an advantage to have a guy like Podsednik on base."

Craig Counsell batted behind Podsednik with the Brewers in 2004 and hit .241 in 140 games, the fourth-lowest average of his nine-year career. Counsell, like Podsednik, is out of Milwaukee now and blossoming this season. Podsednik said he

AVG .290   HR 0   RBI 21   SB 59
AVG .278   HR 15   RBI 75   SB 4

and Counsell spent endless hours talking baseball and discussing strategy for various situations.

"Craig and I were on the same page," Podsednik said. "We knew what the other one was thinking. That is not the case here."

15

Indeed, like some other players in the Sox' international locker room, Iguchi doesn't speak English, which makes it even more amazing the way he and Podsednik have worked so well together.

Iguchi said all that matters to him is doing what is best for the team, but for a player who used to hit in the third hole in Japan, the move to the second spot behind Podsednik offers a different set of problems.

"I do kind of take the first pitch, as well as the first strike, in order to let Pod have a chance to go," Iguchi said. "I will continue to do that because it helps the team. I fall behind on the count a lot of times, but whatever the team needs."

NO PROBLEMS FOR SOX AT GOOD OLD WRIGLEY FIELD

WHITE SOX 5, CUBS 1
MAY 20, 2005
WRIGLEY FIELD

His manager's opinions of Wrigley Field aside, White Sox starter Freddy Garcia might enjoy playing on the North Side more often, given its majority of day games.

"Maybe they should only pitch me in day games," the right-hander said after a 5-1 victory over the Cubs improved his record to 11-1 in his last 15 starts in sunshine.

Maybe another strong showing of timely hitting by his teammates and a struggling six-hit effort from the Cubs were just as relevant.

The combination was good enough to give the Sox a 1-0 lead in the six-game city series, one that seemed to matter most to 38,988 fans if not to Sox manager Ozzie Guillen.

	1	2	3	4	5	6	7	8	9	R	H	E
White Sox	0	0	1	0	3	0	0	1	0	5	10	1
Cubs	0	0	0	0	0	0	1	0	0	1	6	1

White Sox	AB	R	H	RBI	BB	SO
Podsednik, LF	5	1	2	1	0	1
Iguchi, 2B	3	1	1	0	0	0
Rowand, CF	4	0	0	0	0	1
Konerko, 1B	4	0	1	1	0	1
Pierzynski, C	4	0	3	1	0	0
Dye, RF	4	1	2	1	0	0
Uribe, SS	4	0	0	0	0	1
Crede, 3B	4	2	1	1	0	0
Garcia, P	2	0	0	0	0	0
Vizcaino, P	0	0	0	0	0	0
Marte, P	0	0	0	0	0	0
a-Everett, PH	1	0	0	0	0	0
Politte, P	0	0	0	0	0	0
Totals	35	5	10	5	0	4

a-Grounded out for Marte in the 9th.

HR: Crede, Dye; SB: Podsednik; E: Iguchi.

White Sox	IP	H	R	ER	BB	SO
Garcia (W)	7.0	5	1	0	1	3
Vizcaino	0.2	0	0	0	1	0
Marte	0.1	0	0	0	0	1
Politte	1.0	1	0	0	0	0
Totals	9.0	6	1	0	2	4

Cubs	AB	R	H	RBI	BB	SO
Hairston, 2B	5	0	1	1	0	0
Hollandsworth, LF	3	0	0	0	1	1
Lee, 1B	3	0	0	0	0	0
Burnitz, RF	3	0	1	0	1	0
Ramirez, 3B	4	0	1	0	0	1
Patterson, CF	4	0	1	0	0	2
Perez, SS	4	0	2	0	0	0
Blanco, C	4	1	0	0	0	0
Maddux, P	2	0	0	0	0	0
a-Grieve, PH	1	0	0	0	0	0
Remlinger, P	0	0	0	0	0	0
Borowski, P	0	0	0	0	0	0
b-Wilson, PH	1	0	0	0	0	0
Totals	34	1	6	1	2	4

a-Grounded out for Maddux in the 7th. b-Lined out for Borowski in the 9th.

E: Lee.

Cubs	IP	H	R	ER	BB	SO
Maddux (L)	7.0	9	4	3	0	1
Remlinger	1.0	1	1	1	0	2
Borowski	1.0	0	0	0	0	1
Totals	9.0	10	5	4	0	4

HBP: Lee (by Garcia), Iguchi (by Maddux); T: 2:28; Att: 38,988.

A.J. Pierzynski tries to break up Cubs second baseman Jerry Hairston Jr.'s double play with an aggressive slide in the second inning. Photo by Jon Sall/Sun-Times

"The way I look at it, honestly, no," he said of the significance of defeating the Cubs. "Maybe the players get caught up in it because it's the Cubs-Sox, and it's nice to play when there are a lot of people in the stands. That will pump you up.

"But we can't change. I don't care who we play. We have to play our game."

That game is hitting and running and taking advantage of opponents' mistakes, and the formula jelled in the third against Greg Maddux (2-2)

Sox starter Freddy Garcia heads for the dugout after retiring the side. Photo by Jon Sall/Sun-Times

But the worst of it for Maddux came in the fifth, when Crede led off with a wind-defying home run, and his teammates followed with four singles, starting with Podsednik's bunt, in a three-run inning.

The Sox finished their scoring with a two-out homer from Jermaine Dye off Mike Remlinger in the eighth.

"When Derrek Lee hit that ball [to deep center field in the third], I didn't think anyone would hit it out," Guillen said. "Crede crushed that ball. Hopefully, he can continue to do that."

The third baseman had been struggling, but Crede has nothing on the Cubs, who added to their woeful performance with runners on base by stranding nine, though only two reached second base.

The Cubs' only run came in the seventh, when Henry Blanco reached after second baseman Tadahito Iguchi dropped his tailing pop fly. Blanco later scored the unearned run on Jerry Hairston Jr.'s single.

"Maybe you need to pitch better," Maddux said when asked about his team's anemic offense. "It's a lot easier to do that than to hit better.

"I felt I pitched just good enough to lose today."

Garcia pitched more than well enough to succeed, inducing the Cubs to hit nine harmless fly balls and ground into nine outs while striking out three in seven innings.

"Freddy looked like he had a pretty easy day of it, mixing up his breaking ball and locating his fastball," Cubs manager Dusty Baker said.

"He was great, not walking people and getting behind [in counts]," Guillen said. "Today was the Freddy I've seen before."

Aggressiveness was Garcia's key, catcher A.J. Pierzynski said.

"He was more aggressive over the plate, and there was no messing around today," said Pierzynski, who saw his home-run streak end at four games, hitting three singles with an RBI. "He was coming right after guys, getting strike one, and when he does that, you see the results."

At first, though, Maddux and Garcia flirted with unintentional trouble when Maddux hit second batter Iguchi in the first, and Garcia

when first baseman Derrek Lee made a rare error on a Joe Crede ground ball. Garcia (4-3) sacrificed Crede to second before Scott Podsednik followed with a two-out, RBI single.

The Sox congratulate one another after beating the North Siders, 5-1, at Wrigley. Photo by Jon Sall/Sun-Times

plunked Lee with two outs in the bottom of the inning.

Home-plate umpire Fieldin Culbreth immediately warned both teams about beanballs, though the pitchers and managers mildly protested lack of intent.

"They're just doing what they have to do," Maddux said. "I know I didn't hit [Iguchi] on purpose. I don't think it really affected how either one of us pitched the rest of the game."

Garcia professed innocence as well.

"You have to pitch tight," he said. "I wasn't trying to hit anybody. They warned us, and sometimes they have to do this. Maybe because of the excitement, maybe because of all the people screaming."

Baker joined Guillen in a brief discussion with Culbreth, but both sides downplayed the matter afterward.

"They have to protect the players, and if the umpire sees something he thinks is funny, they'll [warn]," Guillen said. "They just said we have to stop this, and I said stop what? But they have a job to do."

Pierzynski understood the umpire's concerns.

"Tensions were high, excitement was high, and two guys get hit," he said. "The umps want to get control. The pitchers weren't trying to hit anyone, but Freddy has a tendency to get wild."

Knowing Maddux, Pierzynski knew Iguchi also wasn't an intentional victim.

"Maddux is always tough," he said. "He won his 300th game against us last year when I was with San Francisco, and he's the same. You have to try to get a ball up against Greg. It's one of those things where you have to be patient. He nibbles, and you have to be patient."

—Written by Toni Ginnetti

JOSE CONTRERAS

No Longer All Over the Map

By Doug Padilla

Escaped from Cuba, defected while in Mexico, reborn in the United States, shipped out of New York and resurrected in Chicago, Jose Contreras now looks to have it all mapped out. The best pitcher going on the White Sox staff isn't so much worried about where he has been to this point. It's all about where he wants to go, and how he will need to keep performing at a high level to help his team get there. Only then will he be able to celebrate with all the flavors of home. A Cuban cigar probably will taste the sweetest after a Sox championship.

"The biggest honor, first of all, is to make the playoffs," Contreras said through interpreter Ozzie Guillen Jr., the manager's son. "It wasn't that long ago, but when we walked in for that first day of spring training, you work out on that first day to have a chance to be in the playoffs and to have a chance at the World Series.

"It's just an honor to be on the team, and it's an honor regardless of where I pitch. It's like being in the main event of a big fight. You have the ball, and it's playoff atmosphere. I want to be on the grand stage. I've pitched in amateur sports, and the biggest honor there is the Olympic Games. The playoffs are much better than that, and I'm just honored to be in the position."

The 2005 season started with the same questions that had plagued Contreras during his brief tenure with the Yankees. Throw more strikes, the Yankees said. The Sox have repeated the sentiment. Throw more fastballs, the Yankees said. The Sox have said the same. Don't be so reliant on your forkball, the Yankees said. The Sox have made the same plea. It just took a while for Contreras to believe what he was being told. He doesn't operate on theories but hard proof.

"I don't think I've ever seen that," Freddy Garcia said about Contreras's remarkable second-half turnaround. "He's been great for us in the second half. He's carried the team. That was big for us.

"For me, it's not a surprise. I know he had a chance to come through, and he has a lot of confidence. He throws his stuff and trusts the people playing behind him. We talk a lot. He's throwing a lot of strikes, and he's not afraid to throw the fastball anymore."

Talking a lot might have been the key for Contreras. The Sox are loaded with Spanish-speaking players, including Garcia, Damaso Marte, Juan Uribe, Pablo Ozuna and Luis Vizcaino. Then there's Contreras's friend and countryman Orlando Hernandez, who has been a steadying influence. No matter how Hernandez pitched this season, he might have earned his keep most by being there every step of the way for Contreras. Still, the biggest steadying influence might be manager Ozzie Guillen. The two speak often, and Guillen says Contreras not only has the best arm on the Sox, but also is the best comedian, hands down. The personal touches cannot be underestimated. It's the difference between Chicago and New York.

"I've been honored to play for two great managers," Contreras said. "They are very

IP 204.2   W 15   L 7   ERA 3.61

different but are two great managers. When I was in New York, I played for Joe [Torre], but with the language barrier, I didn't get to know him personally.

"But with Ozzie, he's my friend on and off the field. I get to talk to him all the time, and we are close friends. He is a great manager and one of the biggest reasons that I am here."

One of the biggest reasons the Sox are where they are, Guillen says, is Contreras's tenacity.

"He has had to compete since he was a baby, and for a lot of different reasons," Guillen said, referring to Contreras's upbringing in Cuba. "He's so quiet, but when he goes to the mound, he's a different man because he likes to compete. "He was [up] against the odds when he was younger, and that's the best way to think about it. He's a competitor, but he is always the funniest guy on the team. He is always joking, talking about his life in Cuba, always with a joke. When you see such a big, quiet man who knows how to tell a joke, it makes you laugh even more."

Photo by Jon Sall/Sun-Times

NO SWEAT FOR WHITE-HOT SOX

WHITE SOX 12, CUBS 2
JUNE 24, 2005
U.S. CELLULAR FIELD

There's no easy way to beat the White Sox, who can pitch, hit, hit for power, run and catch the ball. But the Sox have a way of getting opponents to beat themselves, too—a trap the Cubs seem to be falling into ever more frequently. The season's largest crowd (39,610) at U.S. Cellular Field saw both factors on display as the Sox crushed the Cubs 12-2 with every weapon in their best-in-baseball arsenal.

There were home runs from Frank Thomas, A.J. Pierzynski and Joe Crede among the Sox' 13 hits, and a masterful job from starter Freddy Garcia, who improved to 7-3 overall and 3-0 lifetime (0.82 ERA) against the Cubs with seven innings of one-run, three-hit ball and eight strikeouts. But the Sox gladly accepted the help of six walks from Cubs pitching as well as two wild pitches that allowed a pair of early runs to score.

	1	2	3	4	5	6	7	8	9	R	H	E
Cubs	0	0	1	0	0	0	0	1	0	2	5	0
White Sox	1	0	2	0	5	0	4	0	X	12	13	0

Cubs	AB	R	H	RBI	BB	SO
Patterson, CF	4	0	1	0	0	2
Perez, SS	4	0	0	0	0	1
Lee, 1B	3	0	0	0	0	1
Wilson, 1B	1	0	1	0	0	0
Burnitz, RF	3	0	0	0	1	1
Ramirez, 3B	3	0	1	0	0	0
Macias, 3B	1	0	0	0	0	1
Walker, 2B	2	0	0	0	1	0
Hairston, 2B	1	0	0	0	0	0
Barrett, C	3	0	0	0	0	2
Hollandsworth, LF	3	1	1	1	0	0
Dubois, DH	3	1	1	1	0	2
Totals	31	2	5	2	2	10

2B: Wilson; HR: Hollandsworth, Dubois; SB: Patterson.

Cubs	IP	H	R	ER	BB	SO
Mitre (L)	4.2	7	7	7	4	2
Wellemeyer	2.1	6	5	5	2	2
Borowski	1.0	0	0	0	0	2
Totals	8.0	13	12	12	6	6

White Sox	AB	R	H	RBI	BB	SO
Podsednik, LF	1	2	1	0	3	0
a-Perez, PH-LF	1	0	0	0	0	0
Iguchi, 2B	3	1	2	1	1	1
Thomas, DH	2	1	1	2	1	0
b-Harris, PH-DH	1	0	0	0	0	1
Konerko, 1B	4	0	0	0	1	0
Rowand, CF	5	2	3	1	0	2
Dye, RF	5	2	2	0	0	1
Pierzynski, C	4	2	2	3	0	0
Crede, 3B	4	1	1	3	0	0
Ozuna, SS	4	1	1	0	0	1
Totals	34	12	13	10	6	6

a-Grounded out for Podsednik in the 7th. b-Struck out for Thomas in the 7th.

2B: Pierzynski; HR: Thomas, Pierzynski, Crede; SB: Rowand, Podsednik 2.

White Sox	IP	H	R	ER	BB	SO
Garcia (W)	7.0	3	1	1	1	8
Cotts	1.0	1	1	1	0	1
Vizcaino	1.0	1	0	0	1	1
Totals	9.0	5	2	2	2	10

T: 2:42; Att: 39,610.

Aaron Rowand slides home safely on a wild pitch by Cubs pitcher Todd Wellemeyer. Photo by Scott Stewart/Sun-Times

"If we're going to beat those guys, we have to do it in a big way because you look at their lineup—Aramis Ramirez and Derrek Lee and Jeromy Burnitz—if they have men on base, it's pretty scary," Sox manager Ozzie Guillen said.

No Cubs-Sox game has had a larger margin of victory. And by winning their eighth straight game for the third time this season, the Sox became baseball's first team to reach the 50-win mark (50-22).

"It doesn't mean anything until we get to the postseason," said Pierzynski, who with 11 already has tied his career-high homer mark in a season.

"If we do, then it will mean something. You have to keep it going and find a way to get to the playoffs." Garcia helped lead this journey over Cubs starter Sergio Mitre (2-3), improving his record in day games to 12-1 over his last 17 despite a 5-8 home record over his previous 19 home starts.

"Freddy likes big games," Guillen said.

"In games like this, you get a little more excited and you try to do good," Garcia said. "For me, I don't really do really good in this ballpark. That changed today."

Mitre twice walked leadoff man Scott Podsednik, the major-league base-stealing leader, and Wellemeyer did it once. Mitre picked off Podsednik in the first, but Podsednik singled and stole two bases in the third before crossing the plate on a Mitre wild pitch. Podsednik charged the Sox attack again in the fifth with a lead-off walk in what turned out to be a game-breaking, five-run inning.

"We had a lot of walks," Cubs manager Dusty Baker said. "Especially when you walk Podsednik several times. They have a lot of speed at the top of the order, and that's a recipe for disaster. We didn't have many things working today."

Including a longer outing from Mitre, who lasted only 4-2/3 innings at a time when the battered Cubs bullpen needed better.

"It was pretty beat up in Milwaukee where the Cubs split a four-game series, and we have two more games before an off day," Baker said.

Sox catcher A.J. Pierzynski makes a valiant effort to snag a pop up by the stands, eventually falling over the wall near former Illinois Gov. Jim Thompson (seated, in hat).

Photo by Scott Stewart/Sun-Times

"Sometimes you have to leave somebody out there to save somebody."

That meant enduring a fifth-inning assault that was a textbook demonstration of all that is right about the Sox. It started with Podsednik's walk and ended with Pierzynski's two out, two-run homer off Wellemeyer, who had just entered and wild-pitched Aaron Rowand home. But the bigger key to the inning was Tadahito Iguchi singling, then taking off for second with Paul Konerko batting with one out. Konerko grounded out for the second out of the inning, but Iguchi kept the Sox out of a double play.

"That was a big play to me because it would have been a double play to end the inning, but it kept the rally going," Guillen said. "He was running on his own, but I wanted them to run because I thought we could take advantage of Mitre running. A lot of people don't look at those little things. They look at home runs and numbers, but I told my players because of that play by Iguchi, we scored four more runs."

Guillen's guile was just as duly noted.

"Their manager really knows the game very well," Cubs second baseman Todd Walker said. "There were a couple examples today where he took advantage of us."

The Cubs' only runs came from solo home runs by Todd Hollandsworth in the third, which briefly tied the game after Thomas's first-inning home run, and Jason Dubois in the eighth off Neal Cotts. That was the first homer of the season allowed by Cotts, ending a string of 13-2/3 scoreless innings— yet another sign of the Sox' success.

"They're just all-around solid," Walker said. "They hit home runs, they move runners and they pitch well. That's why they have the record they do."

—Written by Toni Ginnetti

Frank Thomas unloads a home run blast to give the Sox a 1-0 lead in the first inning. Photo by Scott Stewart/Sun-Times

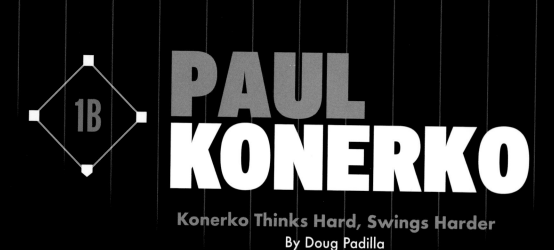

PAUL KONERKO

Konerko Thinks Hard, Swings Harder
By Doug Padilla

Clean-cut, tirelessly prepared and well spoken is the image Paul Konerko projects. Members of the White Sox know there is a darker side. Sometimes Konerko is wrapped in frustration and anger. He has been known to dissect a failed at-bat so thoroughly that teammates and coaches sometimes dread where Konerko will sit after a strikeout, for fear they will have to relive every last detail of what they just watched.

"I don't want to hear his [garbage] when he strikes out," manager Ozzie Guillen said. "I don't want to hear that. He puts so much pressure on himself. There was only one time I said, 'I don't want to hear that.'"

Truth is, when Konerko makes the rare trip to his darker side, it is only to make things brighter. For every step backward, Konerko probably takes 20 forward and the end result leaves him miles ahead of others.

"I never criticize someone who second-guesses himself because that's how you get better, second-guessing yourself," Guillen finally reasoned.

Konerko is the White Sox' man with a plan. Everything seems to have its purpose and it typically is done so even-keel. Even when it is not so level-headed, it is with the purpose of getting back there at some point and usually soon.

"When I first got here three years ago, [hitting guru] Walter Hriniak told me—and Walt's famous for doing this—Walt said you have to tell this guy to just shut up and go hit," Sox hitting coach Greg Walker said. "I've been around Walt enough to know that sometimes that works. But after being around Paul so much, I realized that this guy is so smart to start with and he analyzes—but he analyzes with a purpose.

Praised for his consistency, Konerko actually started in a hole this season and pushed himself to get better each month. It was as if he challenged himself to get better day by day, and the numbers show he succeeded. Over the first month of the 2005 season, Konerko batted a miserable .218, but did contribute seven home runs and 17 RBI. Then in May, Konerko improved slightly with a .227 batting average. And as the summer warmed, so did the Sox' slugger. Konerko batted .293 in June, .315 in July, slipped back to a respectable .300 in August and closed the final month with a .336 average when the Sox needed him most.

"The thing, other than the big numbers he puts up, I just like the way he handled the pressure down the stretch," Walker said. "And that doesn't mean just results. He got results, great. But I'm talking about being on the bench, being MVP-type guy with a focus. He kind of set the tone for us."

The latest view of Konerko has been as a hero.

"Konerko is a superstar, a real superstar," Guillen said. "He's a superstar because he shows up here every day the same way. He goes by the team rules and is just another guy. That's truly a superstar. He plays the game properly. He plays hard. He doesn't put himself in front of anybody. He's here for the team."

AVG | .283   HR | 40   RBI | 100   SLG | .534

And after all these years of being a guy who leads by example, Konerko has started to get more vocal. His leadership has taken all forms.

"Aside from his steady demeanor the last few years we've been together playing here, this season he's definitely come into the forefront as far as in the dugout and getting guys going and emotionally and stuff like that," teammate Aaron Rowand said. "And that's a side of him that I haven't seen a whole lot of since I've been here.

"When we were coming down the stretch and when we've been in big situations like we have been lately, he's definitely been stepping forward and doing more as a leader on this team. It's a big testament to him and it's definitely helping this ballclub to get to where it wants to go."

But for how long?

"To be honest, I wouldn't want to have to think about replacing him," Walker said. "He's such a big part of this team and we've been together for three years, I wouldn't want to think about that."

Photo by Tom Cruze/Sun-Times

SOXKNUCKLEDOWN FORWIN

WHITE SOX 8, RED SOX 4
JULY 22, 2005
U.S. CELLULAR FIELD

Fans wondered if the changed White Sox, who had been among baseball's top home-run hitting teams, would ever be able to score a run with one swing of the bat in 2005.

They wondered, too, if pitcher Jon Garland's long-promised development would turn a corner.

As they have all season, the Sox gave their answers again.

With three home runs accounting for seven of their eight runs, the Sox helped lift Garland to his 15th victory, tops among major-league pitchers, while gaining an 8-4 victory over the defending world champion Boston Red Sox to end their own three-game skid.

"The way we changed things around, people thought in spring training we wouldn't hit home

	1	2	3	4	5	6	7	8	9	R	H	E
Red Sox	0	0	0	1	0	0	1	0	2	4	9	2
White Sox	0	0	0	1	0	6	1	0	X	8	10	0

Red Sox	AB	R	H	RBI	BB	SO
Damon, CF	4	1	1	1	0	1
Stern, CF	1	1	1	2	0	0
Renteria, SS	4	0	0	0	0	0
Cora, SS	1	0	0	0	0	0
Ortiz, DH	4	0	0	0	1	1
Ramirez, M, LF	2	1	0	0	2	0
Hyzdu, LF	0	0	0	0	0	0
a-Olerud, PH	1	0	0	0	0	0
Nixon, RF	3	0	2	0	1	0
Millar, 1B	3	0	1	1	1	1
Mirabelli, C	4	0	1	0	0	3
Mueller, 3B	4	0	1	0	0	0
Graffanino, 2B	4	1	2	0	0	1
Totals	35	4	9	4	5	7

a-Flied out for Hyzdu in the 9th.

HR: Damon, Stern; E: Mirabelli, Hyzdu.

Red Sox	IP	H	R	ER	BB	SO
Wakefield (L)	5.2	9	7	7	1	2
Myers	0.1	1	1	0	0	1
Gonzalez	2.0	0	0	0	0	0
Totals	8.0	10	8	7	1	3

White Sox	AB	R	H	RBI	BB	SO
Podsednik, LF	4	1	1	0	0	0
Rowand, CF	3	2	2	2	0	0
Everett, DH	4	0	0	0	0	1
Konerko, 1B	4	1	2	0	0	0
Gload, 1B	0	0	0	0	0	0
Pierzynski, C	3	1	1	3	1	0
Crede, 3B	4	1	2	0	0	0
Perez, RF	4	1	1	0	0	0
Uribe, SS	4	1	1	3	0	0
Harris, 2B	3	0	0	0	0	2
Totals	33	8	10	8	1	3

HR: Rowand, Pierzynski, Uribe; SB: Podsednik.

White Sox	IP	H	R	ER	BB	SO
Garland (W)	6.2	7	2	2	3	5
Marte	0.2	0	0	0	1	0
Jenks, B	0.2	0	0	0	0	2
Hermanson	1.0	2	2	2	1	0
Totals	9.0	9	4	4	5	7

T: 2:49; Att: 37,511.

Aaron Rowand trots around the bases after his solo homer in the fourth inning tied the game, 1-1. Photo by Jon Sall/Sun-Times

runs anymore," manager Ozzie Guillen said. "The good thing about it is when we do hit them, there are guys on base."

After Aaron Rowand's solo shot off knuckleballler Tim Wakefield (8-9) tied the game in the fourth, A.J. Pierzynski (13th) and Juan Uribe (eighth) each socked three-run homers in the sixth after two outs, chasing Wakefield and enabling Garland to last long enough for the victory.

"Wakefield is a guy you can't explain unless you stand there against him," Pierzynski said of the veteran Red Sox starter. "I fouled off some tough [knuckleballs] and, lucky for me, he made a mistake. I think I heard the whole crowd give a sigh of relief."

Pierzynski's drive broke the tension for 37,511 before Uribe's blast after singles by Joe Crede and Timo Perez provided insurance.

Starting Sox pitcher Jon Garland held the defending world champion Red Sox to just two runs in 6-2/3 innings.
Photo by Jon Sall/Sun-Times

"It got away in a hurry," Boston manager Terry Francona said. "Pierzynski's at bat, we're in a 1-1 game and Wakefield looked terrific. He fouled off some good pitches and finally got to one. Before you know it, they spread it out."

The victory ended a seven-game win streak by the Red Sox in U.S. Cellular Field, a span in which Boston had outscored the Sox 43-26. It also ended a three-game losing streak for the Sox, who regained an 11-game lead over the Minnesota Twins in the American League Central.

"We bounced back," Guillen said. "When we've been down, we get up quickly."

Garland managed to keep Ramirez in check for the most part, though he walked him twice, the second time leading to the Red Sox' first run.

"I was trying to match Wakefield," Garland said. "I saw some of the swings our guys were taking and his ball was dancing. I just wanted to keep us in the game and that's why I was frustrated when I walked Manny and he scored. But Aaron picked me up."

The Red Sox threatened in the fourth, fifth and sixth innings, but Garland escaped each time and limited the scoring to one run in the fourth. The only other run against him came on Johnny Damon's solo homer (sixth) in the seventh.

When Garland retired Edgar Renteria for the second out in the seventh and a pitch count of 117, Guillen ended his outing.

"I was still pretty fired up," said Garland, who exited to a loud ovation. It was good to see the fans coming out and supporting us."

Relievers Damaso Marte and Bobby Jenks held the Red Sox in check, but Dustin Hermanson, who is dealing with back problems, gave up a two-run home run to rookie Adam Stern in the ninth, Stern's first major-league homer. Hermanson walked David Ortiz before pinch hitter John Olerud flied out to end the game.

Garland's season has been as impressive as his team's.

His ERA of 3.19 is fourth-best in the league while his victory total already has surpassed his career best of 12 victories, achieved in each of the three previous seasons.

"I've always had [confidence] in myself," Garland said. "There are a lot of people who don't think it. Things are coming together. I'm making the right pitch at the right time, getting runs when runs are needed and timely defense."

—Written by Toni Ginnetti

Scott Podsednik steals second in the bottom of the seventh in front of second baseman Tony Graffanino, who is unable to get a glove on the ball. Podsednik advanced to third on the play. Photo by Jon Sall/Sun-Times

JON GARLAND

Garland Had It All Along
By Carol Slezak

You thought you knew Jon Garland. He was the California surfer boy who was too laid-back. He was the former first-round draft pick who lacked an inner fire. He was the pitcher with the great right arm and the so-so heart.

You thought you knew Garland, but you were wrong. In fact, you still don't know him. But you're beginning to figure him out.

"People in Chicago probably think he doesn't have a pulse," said Garland's mom, Vikki, from her home in California's San Fernando Valley. "But there isn't anybody more frustrated than him when he doesn't do well. They say he's not aggressive, and I'm thinking, 'C'mon, people. It's the way you interpret things.' I've told Jon it's a double-edged sword. When you're young, they'll say you're too quiet and not aggressive enough. When you get older and have some success, they'll say you have so much poise. You just have to ride it out. It will turn around."

In this case, Mom knew best. After his first five seasons in the major leagues, Garland's record stood at 46-51. He was labeled an underachiever, was booed by White Sox fans and struggled to finish games—often falling victim to the big inning and an early hook. But this season, Garland has turned it around big time.

"My stuff hasn't changed, but I feel a bit more confident out there," Garland said. "The more experience you get, the more your confidence grows."

Garland's success might have surprised all of baseball, but those who know him best aren't surprised a bit.

"You have to wait it out until you reach that point where you say, I belong here,'" said Vikki, who knows her son better than anyone.

After divorcing her husband when Jon was 3, Vikki raised Jon and his two older sisters, Kim and Kerri, alone. Vikki, a former high school athlete, worked long days at her father's medical prosthesis company, yet always made time to play sports with her kids. For Jon, that meant having his own personal baseball coach.

"I give my mom all the credit," Garland said. "For teaching me how to play, for my drive, for everything."

Vikki encouraged her kids to rely on each other when they were young, and they remain a tight-knit bunch today. Kim, 31, and Kerri, 28, make annual trips to Chicago to watch their brother pitch, and when the White Sox visit the West Coast, it becomes a family affair as relatives and friends by the dozen attend the Sox' games. When they can't see Jon in person, there is the baseball package, ESPN and TiVo. Fortunately, there also are cell phones.

Vikki talks to her son several times a week. She always talks to him after he pitches.

"Here's the drill," she said. "After a good outing, I'll call and leave a message on his cell phone, and he'll call back that night or the next day. After a bad outing, I'll call and try to leave him a positive message. He'll call me right back and say, 'OK, what do you got for me?'"

IP | 221.0   W | 18   L | 10   ERA | 3.50

Garland is accustomed to her coaching tips, and they're not all about baseball. When Vikki coached his Pony League team, she told the boys, "Go ahead and tease each other. That's no problem. Just don't ever say, 'You throw like a girl,' or 'You run like a girl.' If you throw bad or run bad, it's because you suck. Don't blame it on girls."

His family suspects that people who don't know him confuse Garland's placid demeanor with a lack of competitiveness.

"People think he doesn't care," Vikki said. "But he's always been very controlled with his emotions. He's quiet and shy, and he comes by it naturally, from me."

During one outing in 2004, Garland was jeered by fans at U.S. Cellular Field. When he was leaving the field, he tipped his cap to the crowd. It was one of the few times he has shown his feelings in such a demonstrative way.

"People in Chicago don't think Jon has a sense of humor," Vikki said. "But when everybody was booing him and he tipped his cap, I thought that was funny. It was his way of saying, 'Yeah, you're right, I stunk.' If fans are going to dish it out, they have to take it."

Garland approaches interviews without much enthusiasm, perhaps heeding his mom's advice to "always keep a little bit of himself for himself" and "don't give everything away" because "it will come back to bite you in the rear." But he would like Sox fans to know one thing about him.

"I'm competitive when I'm on the mound," he said. "To me, that's what it's about, giving 110 percent. That's what I'm doing, even if it doesn't look like it."

Now that you know Garland a little better, you should have no problem believing that.

HOT SOX STICK UP FOR THEMSELVES

WHITE SOX 6, ORIOLES 3
AUGUST 1, 2005
CAMDEN YARDS

Against an opponent riddled with dissension and turmoil, the White Sox banded together for their most unified victory of the season.

After Miguel Tejada aired out his Baltimore Orioles teammates on the bench, the Orioles learned that Rafael Palmeiro had been suspended 10 days for a violation of baseball's new drug policy. Then, for the second game in a row, an Orioles pitcher appeared to throw intentionally at a Sox player.

So Mark Buehrle might have made the biggest sacrifice of all for his teammates when he plunked B.J. Surhoff with a pitch in the sixth inning after A.J. Pierzynski was hit a half-inning earlier. Buehrle's subsequent ejection, the first of his career, ended his streak of pitching at least six innings at 49 starts, but the Sox still completed a four-game sweep—their second on the road since the All-Star break—with a 6-3 victory.

With Sox manager Ozzie Guillen already angry that Tadahito Iguchi was hit by a pitch earli-

	1	2	3	4	5	6	7	8	9	R	H	E
White Sox	1	0	0	0	0	1	1	3	0	6	11	1
Orioles	0	1	0	0	0	0	0	2	0	3	10	0

White Sox	AB	R	H	RBI	BB	SO
Perez, LF	3	1	1	1	2	0
Ozuna, 2B	5	0	1	2	0	1
Everett, DH	4	1	2	1	1	0
Konerko, 1B	4	0	0	0	1	3
Pierzynski, C	3	1	1	1	1	1
Dye, RF	5	1	3	1	0	1
Rowand, CF	5	0	2	0	0	1
Crede, 3B	4	1	1	0	0	1
Uribe, SS	2	1	0	0	1	0
Totals	35	6	11	6	6	8

Orioles	AB	R	H	RBI	BB	SO
Roberts, 2B	5	0	1	0	0	2
Byrnes, LF	5	0	2	0	0	0
Mora, 3B	5	0	0	0	0	1
Tejada, SS	4	0	0	0	1	0
J. Lopez, C	4	1	1	0	0	1
Sosa, DH	4	1	1	0	0	1
Surhoff, RF	3	1	3	1	0	0
Gomez, 1B	4	0	1	0	0	1
Newhan, CF	3	0	1	2	1	1
Totals	37	3	10	3	2	7

2B: Perez, Ozuna, Dye; HR: Pierzynski; E: Ozuna.

2B: Surhoff, Newhan; 3B: J. Lopez; SB: Newhan.

White Sox	IP	H	R	ER	BB	SO
Buehrle (W)	5.2	5	1	0	1	3
Vizcaino	0.1	0	0	0	0	1
Cotts	0.1	0	0	0	1	0
Politte	1.1	1	1	1	0	1
Marte	0.1	3	1	1	0	1
Hermanson (S)	1.0	1	0	0	0	1
Totals	9.0	10	3	2	2	7

Orioles	IP	H	R	ER	BB	SO
Cabrera (L)	6.1	5	3	3	3	5
Byrdak	0.1	1	0	0	1	0
Julio	0.1	3	2	2	0	0
Grimsley	1.0	1	1	1	2	0
Ryan	1.0	1	0	0	0	3
Totals	9.0	11	6	6	6	8

HBP: Surhoff (by Buehrle), Pierzynski (by Cabrera); T: 3:09; Att: 47,823.

Ozzie Guillen and Mark Buerhle argue with umpire Brian Gorman after Buerhle was ejected without warning in the sixth for hitting Orioles batter B.J. Surhoff with a pitch. Photo by Rob Leiter/MLB Photos via Getty Images

Sox right fielder Jermaine Dye robs a hit down the line at Camden Yards. Photo by Rob Leiter/MLB Photos via Getty Images

er in the series, Pierzynski took a pitch from Orioles starter Daniel Cabrera off the right elbow pad in the sixth.

In the bottom of the inning, Buerhle recorded two quick outs and seemed to have the prime opportunity for revenge with Sammy Sosa at the plate. But Sosa singled, and Buerhle hit Surhoff instead. Plate umpire Brian Gorman immediately ejected Buerhle despite the face that no warnings had been given.

"I really can't comment on that," Buerhle said. "But, yeah, I was surprised I got tossed. No warn-

ings were issued. We had a guy get hit yesterday; today A.J. gets hit. Obviously people who know baseball know what happened. But the streak had to end at some time, and it ended today."

The last time Buerhle did not last at least six innings of May 5, 2004—coincidentally also at Baltimore. It was the longest streak of its kind since Steve Carlton went 69 starts from 1979 to '82.

The Sox weren't done with revenge. In Pierzynski's next at-bat in the eighth, he crushed a home run to center field, his 16th of the season. Pierzynski was 6-for-10 in the series with two

Shortstop Juan Uribe leaps over the sliding Chris Gomez to make the throw to first. Photo by Rob Leiter/MLB Photos via Getty Images

homers and four RBI and went 11-for-18 on the six-game road trip.

Despite the ejection, Buerhle picked up the victory to improve to 12-4. He gave up five hits and allowed only an unearned run in the second.

As has happened all season, just when the Sox look vulnerable, the suddenly get their act together. Even the newest member of the Sox was impressed while watching from the bench.

"To say the least, yeah, it was unified," infielder Geoff Blum said. "They got big hits when they needed them; they were sticking up for guys. It was

good team baseball. It was fun to watch and fun to be a part of.

"It's been just one day, but they sure are living up to what I heard."

—Written by Doug Padilla

A.J. PIERZYNSKI

The White Sox are A.J. OK

By Carol Slezak

He came to town a branded man. Had he etched the letter "A" into his forehead, everyone would have known what it meant. "A" for annoying, abrasive, aggravating. "A" for A.J., as in A.J. Pierzynski, who was let go by the San Francisco Giants in December 2004 amid reports he couldn't get along with anyone. Word out of San Francisco was so negative that few teams were interested in taking a chance on him, even though he was an All-Star for the Minnesota Twins in 2003.

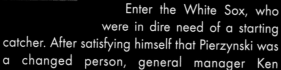

Enter the White Sox, who were in dire need of a starting catcher. After satisfying himself that Pierzynski was a changed person, general manager Ken Williams, who has demonstrated a fondness for acquiring so-called "problem guys"—Roberto Alomar, Royce Clayton and David Wells, for instance—during his nearly five years at the helm, decided to take a chance on Pierzynski.

"I don't feel I've done anything different than I've done in the past," he said. "It was a bad fit for me last year, but here everyone gets along and likes to have fun. And everyone has fair game to say and do what you want, and that's what I like. I like fun atmospheres. It starts with manager Ozzie Guillen and works its way down through the whole team."

"To me, he's one of the funniest guys on this team," Guillen said. "He's a big baby, you know? A big kid who just loves to play the game. Sometimes, maybe he don't like it, but he makes me laugh with the things he does. He doesn't mean to be funny; he's a gamer. Maybe he'll do something to the opponent, and people will hate it, and I just laugh. Like he will try to step on somebody's foot at first base."

Let the record show that Pierzynski has no idea what Guillen is referring to.

"I don't know what I do that people get mad at," he said. "I don't know if I've ever tried to step on someone's foot at first base. I mean, every once in a while I will run across the mound, but that's just because I'm trying to get back to the dugout. But I don't know what I do that everyone talks about. I wish I knew because I'd stop doing it."

Is it such a bad thing to try to get under an opponent's skin?

"Not really," he said. "But when you're trying to find a job and everyone says you're a bad person..."

Pierzynski's experience in San Francisco was the kind that will wound a guy. By comparison, his time with the Sox has been a joy.

"I was lucky from the first day I walked in here," he said. "The guys on this team and the people in the organization welcomed me with open arms and have been great. But it's just one of those things where you never really feel comfortable unless you're Frank Thomas or Paul Konerko or someone like that. For me, coming in to a new team, you know, it's a transition, a work in progress."

"We've had no problems with him," Konerko said. "He's a chippy guy—I mean, you know that going into it—but on the field, there certainly have

AVG .257 HR 18 RBI 56 SLG .420

been no problems at all. He has done great, and he calls a great game."

From Pierzynski's perspective, his Sox teammates are all good.

"It's a lot different than San Francisco because there it was veterans and a little separate," he said. "But here guys all get along and like to be around each other. That's what you look for in a team. Minnesota was similar to that, but this is a little different because Ozzie is out here more. Ozzie is more a part of the team, and that's what you want in a manager. Ozzie understands what it's all about.

"Ozzie makes me laugh because what everyone else wants to say, he's the only one who says it," Pierzynski said. "I think he's great. I think he's awesome."

That is how the Sox approached Pierzynski's arrival, too. They had heard the stories, some of them dating to Pierzynski's time with the Twins. His approach to the game rubbed people the wrong way. He might sulk or become combative when things didn't go his way. But the Sox didn't pre-judge.

"I wasn't worried because I control my team," Guillen said. "A.J. is just another player on the team. I will treat him with respect, I will treat him with loyalty, I will give him some love. The only thing I expect from him is to play the game the way he plays."

Photo by Jon Sall/Sun-Times

ENCORE PERFORMANCE IN BRONX

WHITE SOX 2, YANKEES 1
AUGUST 10, 2005
YANKEE STADIUM

How fitting that a team staying just off Broadway delivered three days of great theater.

The White Sox got the best of the Yankees, capping off a series victory with a dramatic 2-1 matinee triumph in 10 innings before another sell-out crowd. It was the third consecutive low-scoring, one-run game, with the Sox winning by identical scores.

The most recent victory topped even the drama of the night before. The Sox were able to pin a defeat on Yankees closer Mariano Rivera, who is in the midst of a rare Cy Young-caliber season for a reliever. That Juan Uribe and Scott Podsednik turned into heroes on a day in which they had been struggling only added to the wonder.

With one out in the 10th, Uribe crushed a ball into the gap in right-center and immediately realized he needed to turn the hit into a triple at all costs. When center-fielder Bernie Williams tracked the ball at the wall, Uribe was well on his way.

"I knew when I hit the ball that if I got it by Bernie, it would be a triple," said Uribe, whose

	1	2	3	4	5	6	7	8	9	10	R	H	E
White Sox	0	0	1	0	0	0	0	0	0	1	2	5	1
Yankees	1	0	0	0	0	0	0	0	0	0	1	7	0

White Sox	AB	R	H	RBI	BB	SO
Podsednik, LF	5	0	0	1	0	3
Ozuna, 2B	4	1	1	0	1	1
Everett, DH	3	0	1	1	1	0
Konerko, 1B	3	0	0	0	0	0
Rowand, CF	4	0	0	0	0	1
Dye, RF	4	0	2	0	0	0
Blum, 3B	3	0	0	0	1	1
Widger, C	3	0	0	0	0	1
Uribe, SS	4	1	1	0	0	3
Totals	33	2	5	2	3	10

2B: Everett; 3B: Uribe; E: Uribe.

White Sox	IP	H	R	ER	BB	SO
Garcia	8.0	6	1	0	1	5
Cotts (W)	1.1	1	0	0	1	1
Hermanson (S)	0.2	0	0	0	0	1
Totals	10.0	7	1	0	2	7

Yankees	AB	R	H	RBI	BB	SO
Jeter, SS	4	1	1	0	1	2
Cano, 2B	5	0	0	0	0	0
Sheffield, DH	4	0	1	1	0	0
A. Rodriguez, 3B	4	0	1	0	0	1
Matsui, LF	4	0	2	0	0	0
Giambi, 1B	4	0	1	0	0	1
Williams, CF	4	0	0	0	0	1
Flaherty, C	2	0	1	0	0	0
a-Posada, PH-C	2	0	0	0	0	1
Womack, RF	3	0	0	0	0	0
b-Martinez, PH	0	0	0	0	1	0
Crosby, PR	0	0	0	0	0	0
Totals	36	1	7	1	2	7

a-Struck out for Flaherty in the 7th. b-Walked for Womack in the 10th.

Yankees	IP	H	R	ER	BB	SO
Small	7.0	4	1	1	2	7
Gordon	1.0	0	0	0	1	0
Rivera (L)	2.0	1	1	1	0	3
Totals	10.0	5	2	2	3	10

HBP: Konerko (by Small); T: 2:58; Att: 54,635.

Yankees closer Mariano Rivera walks off the mound after giving up the winning hit to Scott Podsednik in the 10th.
Photo by Al Bello/Getty Images

Yankees catcher Jorge Posada can't make the tag as Juan Uribe scores the winning run on Scott Podsednik's 10th-inning infield hit. Photo by Al Bello/Getty Images

first-inning error led to the Yankees' only run. "As soon as I left the box, I was thinking three all the way. I knew it would be harder to score from second off Mariano than it would be to score from third."

Uribe, who had struck out in his first three at-bats, narrowly beat the relay to third. That brought up Podsednik, who also had struck out in his first three at-bats and was 0-for-4 on the day.

On an 0-1 pitch to Podsednik, the Sox tried a suicide squeeze. The bunt rolled foul.

"I thought, 'That's the only chance we can get against Rivera,'" manager Ozzie Guillen said. "This guy has been outstanding."

With the infield in two pitches later, Podsednik hit a grounder between first and second that second baseman Robinson Cano fielded to his left. He straightened up and threw home to get Uribe, who had broken on contact.

On his slide, Uribe was able to push catcher Jorge Posada's left foot backward and score just before the tag. It was the Sox' first run against Rivera since June 24, 2000.

More drama ensued when Neal Cotts walked pinch-hitter Tino Martinez on four pitches with one out in the bottom of the inning. Guillen went to closer Dustin Hermanson, who has been nursing a bad back, and he struck out Derek Jeter for the second out.

Fittingly, the last out was a fly to deep center by Cano that Aaron Rowand tracked down at the warning track. Rowand had made great plays all series, including a catch on the run against Gary Sheffield in the third and another full sprint against Hideki Matsui to end the sixth.

Rowand, who made a strong case for Gold Glove consideration, especially with Minnesota

Sox starter Freddy Garcia sends a pitch to the plate early in the game. Photo by Al Bello/Getty Images

Twins star Torii Hunter out because of an injury, said he never has had a better defensive series.

"There were a lot of opportunities," Rowand said. "It's nice when you get balls hit in areas you can actually catch them. There's a lot of room out there in the gaps in this park to run."

Guillen admitted that be joked on the bench about the Yankees now wanting to acquire Rowand.

"The thing is, this kid doesn't have a name; nobody knows who he is," Guillen said. "But if you see this kid play every day, the way he goes about his business, he should be a Gold Glover."

Sox starter Freddy Garcia sure was appreciative. Like Jose Contreras the day before, Garcia considered the eight-inning outing his best of the season, even though it ended with a no-decision. He didn't give up an earned run and allowed six hits. He had five strikeouts with only one walk.

"I was feeling pretty good. I made my pitches and I got great defense," Garcia said. "Rowand was unbelievable this series. It's all about winning. We find a way to win today, and that's all that matters."

For Guillen, the series helped him learn one more important thing about his team.

"They're just loose," he said. "They just go there and do their job, and we learned we can play under pressure. We can play 1-0 games, 2-1 games against anybody. We can compete against any team."

—Written by Doug Padilla

39

MARK BUEHRLE

Buehrle Slip-Sliding His Way to Greatness

By Doug Padilla

Mark Buehrle, it would seem, lives life like he pitches: in and out of some light trouble with an uncanny ability to rise above the fray.

He is about as open of a book as there is in the White Sox clubhouse, a what-you-see-is-what-you-get guy who is as far from what you would expect from one of baseball's top pitchers.

Buehrle is the Sox' speed-pitching, belly-flopping, ride-bumming, management-worrying superstar who is finally forcing his way into conversations regarding the top left-handed pitchers in the game.

Randy Johnson, Johan Santana, Mark Mulder, Mark Buehrle. Scramble it any way you like. In many lists, Buehrle's name is starting to be listed first.

So what in the name of traffic safety is a guy like Buehrle doing walking a busy Illinois Interstate highway in the middle of the night with his White Sox duffel bag hanging from his prized pitching shoulder?

In a recent effort to find the rare untold story about Buehrle, reliever Neal Cotts won top prize with a gem that makes it obvious as to why Buehrle is a rare breed indeed.

Cotts still laughs at the story now, unsure whether it is even OK to tell it. But after a little soul searching—maybe about 10 seconds—he figures it is something that cannot go untold.

Already somebody he looked up to, Buehrle also added cult-hero status in Cotts' mind that night.

Last season, when Cotts was a rookie, he let it be known that he would be driving to his parents' southern Illinois home for a Monday off day. He would leave right after a Sunday day game at home, spend two nights with the family and return in plenty of time for a Tuesday game. Buehrle, who had yet to purchase his prized German luxury car, needed to get to his St. Louis-area home to get his pickup truck and drive it back to Chicago.

The two headed out on a fairly routine postgame four-hour drive until they neared the point where Cotts would have to go one way and Buehrle the other. So near the I-70, I-55, I-270 junction, Buehrle told Cotts to pull over and leave him somewhere on the side of the road.

Cotts wasn't even sure if Buehrle was serious, but he did have to leave the road to refuel. So at a gas station seemingly in the middle of nowhere, Buehrle grabbed his Sox bag from Cotts's car and called his girlfriend, now his fiancee, Jamie Streck, to make a 30-minute drive to come pick him up.

Cotts insisted that he could take his teammate the rest of the way into the St. Louis area but Buehrle reasoned that the 30 minutes there and the 30 minutes back was unnecessary.

So reluctantly, Cotts got in his car and pulled away, looking in his rearview mirror to see the teammate he admires sitting on a curb, next to the giant Sox logo on his duffel bag. If a Buehrle fan pulled into that gas station that night, not even they would have believed it.

Turns out Streck's directions didn't work out so well, and 30 minutes turned into an hour. Buehrle had since moved to the highway's on-ramp to wait, and getting somewhat impatient, he lifted his bag

IP 236.2   W 16   L 8   ERA 3.12

onto his shoulder and started walking down the highway. Imagine that. It's just hard to picture maybe a guy like Johnson walking down the New Jersey turnpike with a Yankees duffel bag in tow.

Cliff Politte's favorite story was a game against the Minnesota Twins last season when Jacque Jones broke an 0-for-23 slide against Buehrle with a single. The Sox pitcher, at the urging of the Twins bench, offered the ball to Jones at first base for a keepsake. For the record, Buehrle then picked off Jones at first base and struck him out in his remaining three at-bats.

"If I had done it, maybe some-body would have taken it the wrong way and thought I was conceited or thought, 'He thinks he's the man,'" Politte said. "But he's so laid-back and relaxed and easy going that it's funny when he does something like that. It seems like every day he doing something, like the other day he was throwing water in the stands. It's just a pleas-ure to watch."

"I just do what comes natural," Buehrle said. "I try to come in here and have a good time as much as I can. You're going to have your bad days and you're going to have your good days. But when you're in the big leagues making a lot of money playing a game that you love, how could you not be happy every day you come here?"

ALL BIG: VICTORY, INNING, UNIT

WHITE SOX 6, YANKEES 2
AUGUST 21, 2005
U.S. CELLULAR FIELD

None of the White Sox wanted to say the 6-2 victory over the New York Yankees was in the "desperate need" category.

But manager Ozzie Guillen said as much with one word afterward: "Hallelujah!"

Their first victory in the last eight games was more important for the Sox' psyche and that of their fans than it was for the American League standings. They remained 8-1/2 games ahead of the Cleveland Indians in the AL Central with a league-best 75-46 record.

Yet the numbers were starting to creep higher the wrong way, to the point where some at the ballpark were whispering about the 1969 Cubs' August-September collapse.

"The teams behind us are hot, and they already had won," Paul Konerko said of the Indians and Minnesota Twins, the Sox' next opponent. "The pressure's on. If we had lost, we lose another game. We needed that win against some tough odds."

Those odds included facing future Hall of Fame left-hander Randy Johnson—who had dominated the Sox in his years with the Seattle Mariners (11-3, 2.79 ERA)—and trying to end a season-worst seven-game losing streak.

	1	2	3	4	5	6	7	8	9	R	H	E
Yankees	0	0	1	0	0	1	0	0	0	2	11	0
White Sox	0	0	0	6	0	0	0	0	X	6	10	1

Yankees	AB	R	H	RBI	BB	SO
Jeter, SS	4	0	2	0	0	1
Cano, 2B	4	0	1	1	0	0
Sheffield, DH	4	1	2	0	0	0
A. Rodriguez, 3B	4	0	2	0	0	0
Matsui, LF	4	0	1	0	0	1
Williams, CF	4	0	0	0	0	2
Martinez, 1B	4	0	1	1	0	1
Flaherty, C	3	0	0	0	0	0
a-Posada, PH	1	0	0	0	0	0
Womack, RF	4	1	2	0	0	0
Totals	36	2	11	2	0	5

a-Grounded out for Flaherty in the 9th.

2B: A. Rodriguez; SB: Womack.

Yankees	IP	H	R	ER	BB	SO
Johnson (L)	8.0	10	6	6	0	8
Totals	8.0	10	6	6	0	8

White Sox	AB	R	H	RBI	BB	SO
Ozuna, 3B	4	0	2	0	0	0
Crede, 3B	0	0	0	0	0	0
Iguchi, 2B	4	1	1	1	0	2
Rowand, CF	4	1	1	1	0	1
Konerko, DH	4	1	2	1	0	1
Dye, RF	4	1	2	0	0	0
Uribe, SS	3	1	1	0	0	0
Widger, C	3	1	1	3	0	2
Anderson, LF	3	0	0	0	0	2
Blum, 1B	3	0	0	0	0	0
Totals	32	6	10	6	0	8

HR: Iguchi, Rowand, Konerko, Widger; SB: Ozuna; E: Contreras.

White Sox	IP	H	R	ER	BB	SO
Contreras (W)	8.0	11	2	1	0	5
Marte	1.0	0	0	0	0	0
Totals	9.0	11	2	1	0	5

T: 2:18; Att: 39,480.

Tadahito Iguchi touches home plate after hitting the first of three consecutive homers off Yankees starter Randy Johnson in the fourth inning. Aaron Rowand followed with the second home run. Photo by Keith Hale/Sun-Times

One more loss would have given the Sox their first winless homestand of at least six games since 1989. That's why their fourth-inning offensive outburst, featuring four home runs off Johnson (11-8), was so wildly cheered and so tension-breaking.

"You got to where you forget what it feels like [to win]," said Aaron Rowand, who hit the second of three consecutive solo homers in the fourth before Chris Widger capped the inning with a three-run shot. "We were trying too hard, albeit we were playing some good teams. We just hit a bad streak against good teams.

"It was definitely one we needed, just to get back to having fun and feeling good and relaxing.

Starting Sox pitcher Jose Contreras throws against the Yankees early in the game. Contreras allowed 11 hits, but struck out five and had no walks. Photo by Keith Hale/Sun-Times

Guys were pressing, not for themselves but because you wanted to win so much as a unit. I don't think we were having much fun for the last few days. It was a little tense with guys scuffling."

When Sox starter Jose Contreras threw wildly past second base on a failed attempt to pick off Derek Jeter in the third inning, the U.S. Cellular Field crowd of 39,480 collectively winced.

That error, the Sox' seventh in the last eight games, led to an unearned run and a 1-0 deficit.

But the fireworks returned with one out in the fourth when Tadahito Iguchi lined a homer to right field to start the hit parade that had been lacking. Rowand and Paul Konerko followed to make it 3-1 before Jermaine Dye and Juan Uribe singled to set up Widger's blast.

The Sox had scored only two runs in their last 40 innings before the fourth.

"The only thing I could see is bad location, and he kept some pitches up in the strike zone," Yankees manager Joe Torre said of Johnson, who

went on to pitch a complete game. It was a strange game [because] he dominated in seven of the eight innings he pitched."

The Sox hitters agreed, though Contreras turned in his own masterful job despite allowing 11 hits.

"I don't think you can explain it," said Widger, who was 1-for-17 before his homer. "Maybe [Johnson] made a few more mistakes. Maybe we got lucky. Maybe that's what it takes. Other than that one inning, he was tough."

Luck had been absent during the losing streak, but so had sound play, and the Sox were getting criticized for it.

"I don't expect the media to say good things about us when we play badly," Guillen said. "As long as you tell the truth, it's fine by me, and the truth was we weren't playing well."

That was the case again in the third with Contreras's errant throw, the second in as many days by a Sox pitcher. That play bothered Guillen more than a first-inning miscue when Pablo

Third base coach Joey Cora congratulates Paul Konerko after he hit the third of three back-to-back home runs in the fourth inning. Photo by Keith Hale/Sun-Times

Ozuna, who led off with a single and stole second, was picked off by Johnson trying to steal third.

"I don't mind making mistakes if a guy is trying to steal a base because you're being aggressive," Guillen said. "But the [Contreras] play happened two days in a row, and hopefully that will get better."

Guillen had far more praise than criticism for Contreras, who equaled his career high of eight innings and improved to 2-0 with a 1.13 ERA against his former team.

"He has the best stuff in our rotation," Guillen said of Contreras (8-7), who struck out five and had no walks. "He's not the best pitcher, but he has the best stuff."

He also now has the title of stopper.

—Written by Toni Ginnetti

MANAGER

OZZIE GUILLEN

Call-It-a-Career Year For Ozzie?

By Chris De Luca

3

Four more wins, and Ozzie Guillen dissolves into a Venezuelan sunset.

Don't you believe it.

Guillen's threat—it started in spring training and resurfaced at key points throughout the season—is still out there. If the White Sox win the World Series, he just might leave them scrambling for a new manager.

Before the Sox clinched their World Series berth, Guillen revisited the topic of retiring at 41. He was reminded that chairman Jerry Reinsdorf is among the skeptics who believe Guillen is on the south side of serious when he threatens to walk away this winter.

"Well, Jerry is wrong," Guillen said. "If we win this thing, and I get home and say, 'I did what I was supposed to do and I don't want to do it anymore,' then that's what I'll do."

The loquacious Sox manager has no problem expressing his opinion:

On Rangers manager Buck Showalter: "'Mr. Baseball' never even got a hit in Triple-A. He was a backup catcher or a first baseman all his career. Now, all of a sudden, he's the best ever in baseball. ... He told somebody he didn't like me because I have too much fun in baseball. I have fun in baseball because I was good playing this game. And I made a lot of money playing this game ... something he never did."

War of words with Magglio Ordonez: "This is girl [stuff]. Every time there are a couple of [reporters] over there with a piece of paper and a pencil in his hand, is he going to talk about the White Sox? Come on, just move on. Just play you game and forget about the White Sox."

On quitting after winning the World Series: "The way I'm thinking right now, I will tell Kenny Williams to get another manager, and I'll get the [bleep] out of here. I'll make more money signing autographs instead of dealing with this [bleep]."

No way.

This is not to say Guillen is being phony. His words come from the heart.

"When things are going bad," he said, "it can be tough."

Certainly, amid the boos on those lonely walks to the pitcher's mound and the pressure of working in what had been considered a Cubs town in recent decades, Guillen must have drifted off to thoughts of rocking gently on a yacht floating in the Caribbean Sea.

Wake up, Ozzie.

In reality, the decision is out of his hands. If Guillen seriously thinks he can walk away from his dream job to either resurrect his acting career in Venezuelan soap operas or run for mayor of Chicago, he's sadly mistaken.

"If I quit," he said, "I'd have a lot of jobs in a heartbeat."

But not this job. Guillen is the manager of the White Sox. It's not what he does, it's who he is. No one walks away from that.

Jack McKeon, one of Guillen's mentors, would grab him by his red Fire soccer jersey and tell him to get back to work. It's like the mob—you don't just walk away.

"I'm not going to say that's what I'm going to do," he said. "But I have that choice."

It's cute how Guillen thinks he has a choice in all of this.

This team can be more than a one-year wonder. General manager Ken Williams did an excellent job tying up most of his talent through at least next season. There's pressure on everyone who cares deeply about the future of the Sox to keep this thing going. Strip the team, along the lines of letting AL Championship Series MVP Paul Konerko get away, and you become the 1998 Florida Marlins—a World Series winner no one cares about the next season.

Despite a pitching staff overflowing with talent and a lineup that can chip away at any opponent, Guillen is the key to holding all this together. He's the one who pushed for the Sox to take such drastic cuts to the lineup last winter. He's the one who urged Williams to cleanse the clubhouse of malcontents or players whose egos superseded the good of the team.

The *Sporting News*, in a vote among players and managers, announced Guillen as its AL Manager of the Year. In announcing the award, baseball editor Stan McNeal revealed what Indians manager Eric Wedge scribbled about Guillen on his ballot: "He did a tremendous job with the team he has, and he gets the best out of his players."

That's Guillen—getting the best out of his players.

Photo by Jon Sall/Sun-Times

SOX FIND THEIR MO-JOE

WHITE SOX 7 , INDIANS 6
SEPTEMBER 20, 2005
U.S. CELLULAR FIELD

With the bottom of the order now solidified, the White Sox are back to feeling like they can finish on top of the American League Central. No. 9 hitter Joe Crede, who has a history of dramatic home runs, delivered the biggest one of his career in the 10th inning to give the Sox a 7-6 victory over the charging Cleveland Indians and take back a game that nearly slipped away.

The Sox built their division lead back to 3-1/2 games with 12 remaining and dropped their magic number to nine. It is the first time since Sept. 4 that two digits have come off the magic number on the same day because of an Indians defeat and a Sox victory. The home run actually was Crede's second of the game. He has struggled for consistency all season and finally has found it after a recent trip to the disabled list.

	1	2	3	4	5	6	7	8	9	10	R	H	E
Indians	0	2	0	1	0	0	2	0	1	0	6	14	2
White Sox	0	0	2	1	0	0	3	0	0	1	7	11	0

Indians	AB	R	H	RBI	BB	SO
Sizemore, CF	6	0	1	0	0	1
Crisp, LF	6	1	3	0	0	0
Peralta, SS	3	1	1	0	2	0
Hafner, DH	5	1	2	2	0	1
Martinez, C	4	0	1	0	1	2
Gutierrez, PR	0	0	0	0	0	0
Bard, C	0	0	0	0	0	0
Belliard, 2B	5	0	0	1	0	1
Hernandez, 1B	2	1	1	0	1	0
a-Broussard, PH-1B	2	0	0	0	0	1
Boone, 3B	5	1	3	2	0	0
Blake, RF	5	1	2	1	0	2
Totals	43	6	14	6	4	8

a-Popped out for Hernandez in the 8th.

2B: Crisp, Hafner, Martinez; HR: Boone, Hafner, Blake; E: Peralta, Hernandez.

Indians	IP	H	R	ER	BB	SO
Westbrook	6.1	7	4	4	3	4
Howry	0.2	1	2	1	2	0
Betancourt	1.0	0	0	0	0	0
Riske (L)	1.0	3	1	1	0	1
Totals	9.0	11	7	6	5	5

White Sox	AB	R	H	RBI	BB	SO
Podsednik, LF	4	0	0	0	1	0
Iguchi, 2B	5	0	1	0	0	0
Everett, DH	5	1	1	0	0	1
Konerko, 1B	4	2	2	0	1	1
Harris, PR	0	0	0	0	0	0
Gload, 1B	0	0	0	0	0	0
Pierzynski, C	5	1	2	1	0	1
Dye, RF	3	0	1	0	2	1
Rowand, CF	3	0	0	1	0	0
Uribe, SS	4	1	2	1	1	0
Crede, 3B	5	2	2	3	0	1
Totals	38	7	11	6	5	5

2B: Konerko, Everett, Pierzynski; HR: Crede 2.

White Sox	IP	H	R	ER	BB	SO
Buehrle	6.0	7	4	4	2	5
Cotts	0.1	3	1	1	1	0
Politte	1.2	2	0	0	0	0
Jenks	1.0	1	1	1	1	2
Hermanson (W)	1.0	1	0	0	0	1
Totals	10.0	14	6	6	4	8

HBP: Rowand (by Riske); T: 3:31; Att: 26,147.

Joe Crede is mobbed by his teammates after hitting a game-winning home run in the 10th inning.
Photo by Tom Cruze/Sun-Times

While on the shelf with a hairline fracture at the tip of his right middle finger, Crede went to the video room and found new life in a tape of his old batting stance. How fitting that the past returned in a flood as Crede's new-old stance delivered the fifth walk-off home run of his career and the third walk-off home run for the Sox this season. It was the 30th in the history of the new park.

"I've had other walk-off home runs, but they're either really early in the season or we were already out of it," Crede said. "But with the fact that we're in first place and we're in the last week and a half of the season here and we're battling back and forth here, I think it is one of the biggest hits of my career."

Crede's defense at third base always had been appreciated, and now the Sox can give thanks to his offense.

"He's been great since he's come back from the DL," manager Ozzie Guillen said. "I think this kid can carry a team for two or three weeks, he's that good."

He has been doing just that. Yet Crede nearly didn't get a chance at his heroics because of another rally from the blazing-hot Indians, who entered having won six consecutive games and 13-of-their-previous-14.

Mark Buehrle was shaky after giving up four runs, seven hits, and two walks in six innings. He allowed three home runs and said he was lucky to not give up 10. But after the Indians scored two runs in the seventh—one off Buehrle and one off reliever Neal Cotts to take a 5-3 lead—the Sox' offense delivered some clutch hits and got a much-needed break.

Juan Uribe, A.J. Pierzynski and coach Don Cooper confer at the mound with reliever Bobby Jenks.
Photo by Tom Cruze/Sun-Times

The Sox grabbed a 6-5 lead in their half of the seventh by getting a run on an A.J. Pierzynski double and another on an Aaron Rowand sacrifice fly. But as Indians first baseman Jose Hernandez cut off the throw to home on Rowand's sacrifice fly, he tried to cut down Pierzynski advancing to third. The throw went up the left-field line and the Sox had the lead. The Indians then cashed in on a Bobby Jenks leadoff walk in the ninth to tie the score when Ronnie Belliard delivered a run-scoring ground out.

The Sox could have played the infield in with runners on second and third with one out, but Guillen didn't want to give the Indians an easier chance at a hit that would have given them two runs and the lead. Dustin Hermanson (2-4) worked the 10th inning, adding to all the drama when Guillen paid him a visit to check on his ailing back. Hermanson remained in the game.

By the time it ended, Buehrle said he had forgotten all about a poor outing when he was overthrowing and felt lucky to keep the Indians in check.

"Of course I was frustrated when they took the lead 4-3, but as soon as we battled back, it doesn't really matter," Buehrle said. "It doesn't even feel like I pitched. As long as we get the win, it doesn't matter how it happens or what goes on."

—Written by Doug Padilla

Joe Crede launches a walk-off shot in the 10th inning to beat the Indians 7-6. Photo by Tom Cruze/Sun-Times

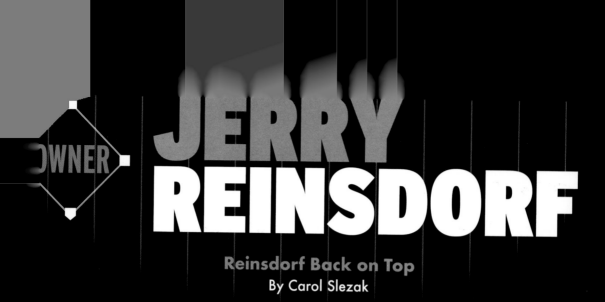

OWNER

JERRY REINSDORF

Reinsdorf Back on Top

By Carol Slezak

f we gripe about Jerry Reinsdorf when his teams are down, then we owe him a pat on the back when his teams are up. Don't we?

"I told him, 'Holy smokes, we're having a good year, you're liable to be popular again,'" Sox vice chairman Eddie Einhorn said.

In lieu of popularity, respect will suffice. And a little fairness never hurts.

"As vitriolic as [the media] have sometimes been in Chicago, that can get you down," Einhorn said. "Especially when you're misrepresented. Jerry can take a hit, but he gets upset when he's misrepresented. And with two teams, you take a double hit."

Reinsdorf has been hit hard by both Bulls and Sox fans over the last several years. With the exception of the 2000 Sox, neither team has made the playoffs since the Bulls' run ended in 1998. But when the Bulls were claiming championships as a birthright, winning six titles during the Michael Jordan era, Reinsdorf didn't get much credit. Win or lose, he can't win.

"Jerry is not one to say, 'I told you so,' but after 25 years, you've got to get pleasure out of [the fact that both the Bulls and Sox are winning]," Einhorn said. "We're all human. He's human. You have to take pleasure, especially after you're getting beaten up all the time."

The public thinks it knows Reinsdorf. He's that stubborn, cheap, cold fellow who owns the Bulls and Sox. He's the guy who stuck with Jerry Krause for too long before bringing in fresh blood with John Paxson. He's the guy who won't spend money on his baseball team. Isn't he?

"The public and the media really don't know [owners] as people," Einhorn said. "They know what they represent. I kid Jerry that if he ever had a fault, it's probably a fault we would all love to have. It's called loyalty. That's a wonderful trait in a human being."

He cares more than you think.

Reinsdorf's human traits aren't always portrayed, at least accurately, according to some who know him on a personal level.

"Most people, for some reason, look at Jerry as a guy who is distant," said Paxson, the Bulls executive vice president of basketball operations. "I've never found him that way."

BROUGHT STABILITY TO BULLS, SOX

Reinsdorf has weathered 24 full seasons as Sox chairman and 20 seasons as Bulls chairman. Sure, he once toyed with the notion of moving the Sox out of state. But he never did.

"He's stabilized two franchises that were not very stable in the history of this city," Einhorn said. "Owners have turned over two or three times in some [baseball] cities since we've been involved with the White Sox. That tells you that deep down he loves it."

Jerry Colangelo, who until last year was also the chairman of baseball's Arizona Diamondbacks, knows how challenging it is to head one organization, let alone two.

"You have to have passion for what you do," Colangelo said. "Jerry falls into that category. He dedicates himself to [the teams]. He spends 99 percent of his time on the teams, and he is very

To be both hands-on and non-interfering is a difficult trick. But, to the great relief of his employees, Reinsdorf has mastered the art.

A NICE GUY WITH A SMALL EGO

Reinsdorf, who rarely grants interviews and wasn't contacted for this story, is by nature a private person. The fact that he doesn't seek publicity likely has had a negative effect on his public image. But he simply isn't interested in celebrity trappings.

"Twenty-five years, he has been terrific," Einhorn said. "I think we've had two arguments that whole time. You certainly see a lot of big egos in sports, but I haven't seen it in him."

When Sox management met after a third straight second-place finish last season, Reinsdorf asked general manager Ken Williams what he wanted to do. Williams said he wanted to get a fifth starter and two arms for the bullpen and to rely less on home runs.

"And Jerry supported Kenny," Einhorn said. "He liked the ideas, we liked them, and he said, 'Let's go with it.'"

While many still are clamoring for a higher Sox payroll, Einhorn believes Reinsdorf is a businessman who is doing the best he can.

"We have spent what we feel is right for our ownership group," Einhorn said. "We have increased payroll [steadily]. But, very honestly, we don't take in the income. And we've seen that spending doesn't guarantee anything. We lost to a team [the Minnesota Twins] three years in a row that spent less than us. So what does money do? But we've put all the money back into the team, and that's a fact."

Here is another fact: Reinsdorf wants to win. How badly does he want to win? So badly that he is not currently sharing the joy of Bulls and Sox fans. He can't. He's afraid he might jinx his teams.

"He's the kind of guy who with two outs in the ninth and a four-run lead will say, 'We haven't won it yet,'" Einhorn said. "That's just the way he is."

"LOOK OUT IN POSTSEASON," KONERKO WARNS

WHITE SOX 4, TIGERS 2
SEPTEMBER 29, 2005
COMERICA PARK

The only choke was manager Ozzie Guillen and general manager Ken Williams choking back tears of joy.

After owning baseball's best record for much of the season, the White Sox had threatened in recent weeks to give away every bit of their double-digit lead in the American League Central. But they found an extra gear to get the job done this week. A 4-2 victory over the Detroit Tigers officially put the Sox in the playoffs and gave them their first division title in five years with a 96-63 record.

The Sox still can finish in a tie for first if they are swept this weekend by the Cleveland Indians, but under that scenario, the Sox would win a tiebreaker based on their winning record against the Indians and would enter the playoffs as division champs; the Indians would go as the wild card. It's the first time the Sox have finished in first place twice in the same decade since 1917 and 1919.

Talk about your brushes with history. The Sox will make their eighth postseason appearance, and

	1	2	3	4	5	6	7	8	9	R	H	E
White Sox	2	1	0	0	0	1	0	0	0	4	10	1
Tigers	0	0	0	0	0	0	1	1	0	2	10	0

White Sox	AB	R	H	RBI	BB	SO
Podsednik, LF	4	0	1	1	0	0
Ozuna, 3B	4	0	2	0	0	0
Crede, 3B	1	0	0	0	0	0
Dye, RF	4	1	1	0	0	0
Konerko, 1B	2	2	2	1	2	0
Everett, DH	4	0	3	2	0	0
Rowand, CF	4	0	0	0	0	0
Pierzynski, C	3	1	1	0	0	0
Uribe, SS	2	0	0	0	0	0
Harris, 2B	2	0	0	0	2	0
Totals	30	4	10	4	4	0

Tigers	AB	R	H	RBI	BB	SO
Granderson, CF	5	0	0	0	0	2
Polanco, 2B	5	1	2	0	0	0
Shelton, DH	4	0	1	0	0	0
Ordonez, RF	4	0	1	1	0	0
Pena, 1B	4	0	1	0	0	2
Monroe, LF	4	1	1	0	0	2
Inge, 3B	4	0	4	0	0	0
Wilson, C	4	0	0	0	0	0
Infante, SS	3	0	0	0	0	1
a-Young, PH	1	0	0	0	0	1
Totals	38	2	10	1	0	8

2B: Dye, Pierzynski; 3B: Everett; HR: Konerko; E: Crede.

a-Struck out for Infante in the 9th.

2B: Ordonez.

White Sox	IP	H	R	ER	BB	SO
Garcia (W)	7.0	8	2	2	0	5
Politte	0.1	1	0	0	0	0
Cotts	0.1	0	0	0	0	1
Jenks (S)	1.1	1	0	0	0	2
Totals	9.0	10	2	2	0	8

Tigers	IP	H	R	ER	BB	SO
Grilli (L)	7.0	8	4	4	2	0
Spurling	1.0	1	0	0	1	0
Rodney	1.0	1	0	0	1	0
Totals	9.0	10	4	4	4	0

HBP: Pierzynski (by Rodney); T: 2:22; Att: 13,494.

A.J. Pierzynski (left), Bobby Jenks (center) and the Chicago White Sox celebrate their division title after beating the Tigers 4-2.
Photo by Tom Cruze/Sun-Times

they haven't won a playoff series since the 1917 World Series.

"A lot of people don't realize how hard it is to get to the playoffs," Guillen said. "Playing in the playoffs is easier than to play all year long and make this thing happen. When you get to the play-offs, it's even-up. Everybody starts over. But that is why you work so hard all year long."

First baseman Paul Konerko, the only starter for both the 2000 and 2005 AL Central champions, helped reel in this title with a sixth-inning home run in support of starter Freddy Garcia (14-8). Konerko's drive over the bullpens in left field gives

him 40 homers in back-to-back seasons. Frank Thomas is the only other Sox player to do that. Konerko, who will be a free agent this offseason, has become somewhat of an unofficial team spokesman lately, handling most of the inquiries regarding a possible Sox collapse down the stretch. With the evaporating lead, questions about the team's playoff worthiness and an overall negative feeling surrounding the Sox for more than a month now, he said the team is transformed with the division title secured.

"It's tough to see around here right now, but I sense this team has a chip on its shoulder,"

Sox first baseman Paul Konerko begins the celebration after catching a liner for the final out.
Photo by Tom Cruze/Sun-Times

Konerko said with a determined voice as corks popped and champagne sprayed all around him in the clubhouse.

"We know we've got the pitching to do something here. With the timely hitting coming around, which it did the last couple days, look out. That's the attitude we have around here. I see this team being very hungry. I see this team being very [ticked] off. That's a good thing."

It was hard to ignore the symbolism in the victory. There was strong pitching from Garcia, a trait that helped the Sox forge their large lead. There was the offense that did just enough—a two-run triple from Carl Everett, a run-scoring fly ball from Scott Podsednik and Konerko's home run supplied all the scoring.

"It was like our season," Konerko said. "We cruised through seven innings, and then we got a little tight at the end and pulled it out."

Garcia, who relishes high-profile games, got one in Detroit of all places. Even without his best stuff, he made the most of it, allowing two runs and eight hits in seven-plus innings. Bobby Jenks got the last four outs for his fourth save.

"We deserve to be here right now celebrating because we were working hard all year long," Garcia said. "As soon as we left spring training, we had a goal, and the goal was to win the division. We did that, and now we have to step up for the first round of the playoffs."

After what the Sox went through this season, they sound like a team that has learned an important lesson.

"To be here right now doing this [celebrating] with these guys, it's amazing," center fielder Aaron Rowand said. "We stuck together and talked about team chemistry when we were winning early on in the year, and everybody said, 'Yeah, well, it's easy when you're winning.' But when you're losing and everybody in the papers is doubting you and all that, everybody still stuck together. And that showed the character of this team."

Williams made character one of his criteria for acquiring players and was convinced that the cele-

The White Sox gather for a team photo on the field at Comerica Park after winning the division title. Photo by Tom Cruze/Sun-Times

bration would not have happened if the players didn't have it. Before, he still had his doubts.

"I was nervous when the lead was 15, that would be an affirmative, yeah," Williams said. "What are you going to do? Are you going to crawl into a hole and are you going to die, or are you going to come out fighting? One of the reasons we picked each one of these guys on this team is we wanted a bunch of fighters. We wanted guys who could be resilient and had been resilient to criticism or doubts throughout the course of their whole career.

"The team as a whole throughout the course of the year, up until today—and you know what, tomorrow, too—it will continue that we will be doubted for various reasons. But it should be a team that people enjoy more. They go about it the right way, and they really care."

—Written by Doug Padilla

AMERICAN LEAGUE DIVISION SERIES

IT'SAROUTTIME

WHITE SOX 14, RED SOX 2
OCTOBER 4, 2005
U.S. CELLULAR FIELD

If the White Sox don't end up winning the World Series, perhaps a Tony Award is in order.

Judging by the amount of curtain calls they received in their 14-2 victory over the Boston Red Sox in Game 1 of the American League Division Series, it might be justified.

A matinee crowd of 40,717 figured to see another dominating pitching performance from Jose Contreras and got so much more. It was as if the understudy was supposed to take over in *The Producers*, and Matthew Broderick returned instead.

The Sox won their first home playoff game since Game 1 of the 1959 World Series against the Los Angeles Dodgers, snapping a nine-game home skid in the postseason. The Sox' triumph also snapped the Red Sox' eight-game postseason win-

	1	2	3	4	5	6	7	8	9	R	H	E
Red Sox	0	0	0	2	0	0	0	0	0	2	9	0
White Sox	5	0	1	2	0	4	0	2	X	14	11	1

Red Sox	AB	R	H	RBI	BB	SO
Damon, CF	4	0	0	0	0	2
Cora, SS	0	0	0	0	0	0
Renteria, SS	4	0	1	0	0	0
Hyzdu, CF	0	0	0	0	0	0
Ortiz, DH	4	0	2	0	0	1
M. Ramirez, LF	4	0	0	0	0	1
Nixon, RF	4	1	2	0	0	0
Varitek, C	4	1	1	0	0	1
Millar, 1B	3	0	1	1	0	1
a-Olerud, PH	1	0	1	0	0	0
Mueller, 3B	4	0	0	0	0	1
Graffanino, 2B	4	0	1	0	0	0
Totals	36	2	9	1	0	6

a-Doubled for Millar in the 9th.

2B: Renteria, Graffanino, Millar, Ortiz, Olerud.

Red Sox	IP	H	R	ER	BB	SO
Clement (L)	3.1	7	8	8	0	0
Bradford	1.1	0	0	0	0	1
Gonzalez	2.1	2	4	4	1	0
Arroyo	1.0	2	2	2	2	1
Totals	8.0	11	14	14	3	2

White Sox	AB	R	H	RBI	BB	SO
Podsednik, LF	3	2	2	3	1	0
Iguchi, 2B	3	0	0	0	0	1
a-Harris, PH-2B	1	0	1	1	0	0
Dye, RF	3	0	0	0	0	0
b-Perez, PH-RF	1	0	0	0	0	0
Konerko, 1B	4	2	1	2	0	0
c-Blum, PH-1B	1	0	0	0	0	0
Everett, DH	4	1	1	0	0	0
Rowand, CF	3	2	1	1	1	0
Pierzynski, C	3	4	3	4	0	0
Crede, 3B	3	1	0	0	1	0
Uribe, SS	4	2	2	3	0	1
Totals	33	14	11	14	3	2

a-Singled for Iguchi in the 8th. b-Flied out for Dye in the 8th. c-Popped out for Konerko in the 8th.

2B: Pierzynski; HR: Pierzynski 2, Konerko, Uribe, Podsednik; SB: Podsednik; E: Crede

White Sox	IP	H	R	ER	BB	SO
Contreras (W)	7.2	8	2	2	0	6
Cotts	0.1	0	0	0	0	0
Politte	1.0	1	0	0	0	0
Totals	9.0	9	2	2	0	6

HBP: Podsednik (by Clement), Dye (by Clement), Pierzynski (by Gonzalez); T: 2:56; Att: 40,717.

A.J. Pierzynski watches his home run ball in the eighth inning, his second homer of the game. The White Sox hit five home runs en route to beating the Red Sox 14-2. Photo by Tom Cruze/Sun-Times

ning streak and their six-game winning streak in the ALDS.

The Sox won their first postseason game since Game 3 of the 1993 American League Championship Series against the Blue Jays, and their 14 runs were seven more than their entire output in the 2000 Division Series against the Mariners.

Contreras did his part by allowing two runs and eight hits in 7-2/3 innings. After returning to the dugout to a standing ovation, he came back to the top step to acknowledge the crowd, one of five curtain calls on the day.

The others were reserved for the offense as home-run hitters A.J. Pierzynski, Paul Konerko,

Juan Uribe and Scott Podsednik all were showered in cheers. The five home runs and 14 runs scored were a Sox record for the postseason. It was also the most home runs hit in a Division Series game by an AL team.

Pierzynski hit the first of his two home runs in a five-run first inning, but it was Konerko in the third to get the first call to the top step from the fans after hitting a line drive into the Sox' bullpen.

"I told somebody on the bench I felt good about that curtain call; I felt great," said Konerko, who then hit the sarcasm button. "Then seven [actually, five] curtain calls later, it wasn't so special. They were handing them out all day."

The offensive explosion was simply too hard to ignore. A Sox team that struggled to score runs all season—and had 35 one-run victories—was pounding Matt Clement. It was as if the former Cub was facing his own offense instead of the one that won 15 games this season even though they scored two runs or less.

"We had some time today, unfortunately, to come to grips with the way the game was going," Red Sox manager Terry Francona said.

The damage started early as the Sox scored those five first-inning runs. The first run came on a Konerko fielder's choice for the second out. Four more followed, including a three-run home run from Pierzynski one pitch after bunting a ball foul.

"It doesn't mean anything for [today]," Pierzynski said, trying to put some perspective on the offensive showing. "These guys aren't going to quit or go away. They've done things that are special. It [just] means we hit five homers. David Wells is going to try to stick it up our rear ends [today], and we have to bring the same intensity and try to do it again."

That would leave it to Mark Buehrle to match the effort of Contreras, who closed out the season by winning his last eight starts. The right-hander was 6-0 in September with a 1.99 ERA.

Injured slugger Frank Thomas waves to the crowd before tossing out the first pitch. Photo by Tom Cruze/Sun-Times

Juan Uribe celebrates as he rounds first base after hitting a fourth-inning, two-run homer off Red Sox starter David Wells.
Photo by Jon Sall/Sun-Times

"I think everybody's focusing on the 14 runs," Konerko said. "I'm focused on the two runs [allowed]. That was the story of the day."

With his family in the stands, Contreras was even more intent on shutting down the Red Sox, who have traditionally caused him problems. In seven previous appearances against the Red Sox, Contreras was 2-4 with an 11.67 ERA.

"My family wasn't here when I pitched [in the playoffs] the first time," Contreras said. "Even though I came out as a reliever [in 2003 with the Yankees], this was my first start. You have that extra support when you see your wife and kids. If you don't go out there and succeed, your family is suffering because they're watching you live."

One of the reasons everything turned out just fine was that Contreras held Johnny Damon, David

Ortiz and Manny Ramirez to two hits in 12 at-bats with no RBI.

"You have those guys in the lineup, and you pray for the best," manager Ozzie Guillen said. "He was throwing strikes. He was throwing quality pitches, and that's what you have to do with that team because they will score in a heartbeat."

Neal Cotts came on for Contreras in the eighth and got a fly out to end the inning. Cliff Politte pitched the ninth and closed out the victory.

"Our pitching staff carried this team all the way, and I still believe they're carrying us," Guillen said. "It's nice to see a lot of guys score a lot of runs because our pitching staff can breathe a little bit."

—Written by Doug Padilla

E-LECTRIFYING WIN FOR WHITE SOX

WHITE SOX 5, RED SOX 4
OCTOBER 5, 2005
U.S. CELLULAR FIELD

Wire to wire or just off the pace, the White Sox seem to have all of the winning scenarios covered.

Tadahito Iguchi—one of the few who didn't deliver in the blowout victory—came up huge in Game 2 with a three-run home run off David Wells to cap a five-run rally in the fifth inning and push the White Sox to a 5-4 victory. While White Sox fans will remember the Iguchi homer and a six-out save from rookie Bobby Jenks, a Tony Graffanino fielding error to extend the inning is destined to go down in Red Sox lore.

It's only the seventh time in the history of the American League Division Series that a team has rallied from four or more runs down for the victory.

The White Sox have a 2-0 lead in the best-of-five ALDS and have moved to within a game of their first playoff series victory since winning the World Series in 1917. And if the White Sox want to to wrap this triumph in even more nostalgia, they have two chances to win the series clincher at historic Fenway Park.

"Don't count on anything," manager Ozzie Guillen cautioned. "I think we have to go there and

	1	2	3	4	5	6	7	8	9	R	H	E
Red Sox	2	0	2	0	0	0	0	0	0	4	9	1
White Sox	0	0	0	0	5	0	0	0	X	5	9	0

Red Sox	AB	R	H	RBI	BB	SO
Damon, CF	5	2	2	0	0	0
Renteria, SS	5	1	2	0	0	0
Ortiz, DH	4	1	1	0	0	1
M. Ramirez, LF	3	0	1	2	1	0
Varitek, C	4	0	2	1	0	0
Nixon, RF	3	0	0	1	1	0
Mueller, 3B	4	0	0	0	0	1
Olerud, 1B	4	0	0	0	0	0
Graffanino, 2B	4	0	1	0	0	0
Totals	36	4	9	4	2	2

2B: Renteria, Ortiz, Graffanino; E: Graffanino.

White Sox	AB	R	H	RBI	BB	SO
Podsednik, LF	4	0	0	0	0	0
Iguchi, 2B	4	1	2	3	0	0
Dye, RF	4	0	1	0	0	1
Konerko, 1B	4	0	1	0	0	0
Everett, DH	4	1	2	0	0	0
Rowand, CF	3	1	1	1	0	0
Pierzynski, C	3	0	0	0	0	0
Crede, 3B	3	1	1	1	0	1
Uribe, SS	3	1	1	0	0	0
Totals	32	5	9	5	0	2

2B: Rowand; HR: Iguchi.

Red Sox	IP	H	R	ER	BB	SO
Wells (L)	6.2	7	5	2	0	2
Papelbon	1.1	2	0	0	0	0
Totals	8.0	9	5	2	0	2

White Sox	IP	H	R	ER	BB	SO
Buehrle (W)	7.0	8	4	4	1	2
Jenks (S)	2.0	1	0	0	1	0
Totals	9.0	9	4	4	2	2

T: 2:29; Att: 40,799.

Joe Crede races to third after Juan Uribe's infield hit went through the legs of Red Sox second baseman Tony Graffanino in the fifth inning. Photo by Jon Sall/Sun-Times

play hard and play the way we play because, believe me, the Boston Red Sox have been there before, and they know how to come out of it. I know they're not panicking. I know they're taking things real easy. Believe me, they will be ready to go when we get to Boston."

Freddy Garcia didn't face the Red Sox during the season. While Garcia has six games of postseason experience, Mark Buehrle was making his first start in the playoffs, and the Red Sox got to him early. The left-hander gave up a single to Johnny Damon to open the game followed by a double to Edgar Renteria to put two runners in scoring position. Both scored on a one-out single by Manny Ramirez, who was hitless in four at-bats in Game 1.

After starting the playoffs with a bang with a five-run first inning, the White Sox went quietly in order against Wells to start Game 2.

The Red Sox, though, were anything but quiet early. They scored two more runs off Buehrle in the third inning on a Jason Varitek single and a run-scoring fielder's choice from Trot Nixon.

The White Sox seemed to have nothing for Wells and his slow curveball until the fifth inning, and even then, it took some breaks to deliver. Carl Everett opened the inning with a single, and Aaron Rowand followed with a bloop double down the left-field line that he initially thought was going to be foul. Everett scored easily to cut the Red Sox' lead to 4-1.

Tadahito Iguchi watches as his fifth-inning, three-run homer puts the White Sox ahead 5-4. Photo by Jon Sall/Sun-Times

Catcher A.J. Pierzynski congratulates closer Bobby Jenks after he held the Red Sox scoreless for the save.
Photo by Tom Cruze/Sun-Times

After a one-out RBI single up the middle by Joe Crede, the White Sox received the break that just might carry them into the AL Championship Series for the first time since 1993 when they fell to the Toronto Blue Jays in six games.

Juan Uribe hit a grounder that Graffanino had to move to his right to field. With an inning-ending double play all laid out for him, the former White Sox utilityman had the ball go through his legs to put runners on the corners.

After Scott Podsednik appeared to spoil a prime scoring opportunity when he fouled out to third base, Iguchi crushed a 1-1 breaking ball into the Sox' bullpen in left to put the White Sox on top.

"I had talked to Greg [Walker], the batting coach, about hitting Wells' curves," Iguchi said through interpreter Ryan McGuire. "All this year I had been fooled by Wells' curves, so I went out trying to hit it today, and I'm happy it happened."

The unlikely scenario brought back memories of the July 21, 2005, game at U.S. Cellular Field, when Crede dropped a Ramirez pop-up in foul territory, and the Red Sox slugger used the new life to deliver the game-winning home run.

At the time of the uprising, Buehrle was in the middle of solving the puzzle that is one of the AL's top offenses. After the third inning, Buehrle retired 12 of the last 14 batters he faced before giving way to Jenks.

"Going back out there after we scored five runs, and to take the lead like that, you wanted to go out there and throw up zeros as quick as you can," Buehrle said. "Then the first guy got on [in the sixth inning], and I said, 'Here we go again.' Once I got taken out, I went over and gave everybody high-fives on the offense and said thanks."

—Written by Doug Padilla

SOXLOWER THEBROOM

WHITE SOX 5, RED SOX 3
OCTOBER 7, 2005
FENWAY PARK

Nearly forced to watch the playoffs unfold from his living-room couch, Orlando Hernandez is feeling pretty wanted now.

The veteran right-hander, who turns 40 in three days, mixed equal parts of guts and etermination to get the White Sox out of a giant mess and into the American League Championship Series with a 5-3 victory over the Boston Red Sox.

The White Sox earned their first ALCS appearance since 1993 with a three-game sweep of the defending World Series champions.

"It feels good to knock off the defending champs, but there are two more better feelings out there," said Sox veteran Paul Konerko, whose two-run home run in the sixth inning supplied the winning runs. "I don't consider it any more special for

	1	2	3	4	5	6	7	8	9	R	H	E
White Sox	0	0	2	0	0	2	0	0	1	5	8	0
Red Sox	0	0	0	2	0	1	0	0	0	3	7	1

White Sox	AB	R	H	RBI	BB	SO
Podsednik, LF	4	1	1	1	0	1
Iguchi, 2B	5	0	1	1	0	2
Dye, RF	3	1	1	0	1	1
Konerko, 1B	4	1	1	2	0	1
Everett, DH	3	0	0	0	0	0
Rowand, CF	4	0	2	0	0	1
Pierzynski, C	3	1	1	0	1	0
Crede, 3B	3	0	0	0	0	0
Uribe, SS	3	1	1	1	0	1
Totals	32	5	8	5	2	7

2B: Uribe, Podsednik, Rowand, Pierzynski; HR: Konerko; SB: Rowand, Pierzynski.

White Sox	IP	H	R	ER	BB	SO
Garcia (W)	5.0	5	3	3	4	1
Marte	0.0	1	0	0	2	0
Hernandez	3.0	1	0	0	0	4
Jenks (S)	1.0	0	0	0	0	1
Totals	9.0	7	3	3	6	6

Red Sox	AB	R	H	RBI	BB	SO
Damon, CF	4	0	1	0	1	2
Renteria, SS	4	0	0	0	1	1
Ortiz, DH	4	1	1	1	0	1
M. Ramirez, LF	3	2	2	2	1	0
Nixon, RF	4	0	1	0	0	1
Mueller, 3B	3	0	0	0	1	0
Olerud, 1B	2	0	1	0	2	0
Machado, PR	0	0	0	0	0	0
Millar, 1B	0	0	0	0	0	0
Mirabelli, C	2	0	0	0	0	0
a-Varitek, PH-C	2	0	0	0	0	1
Graffanino, 2B	4	0	1	0	0	0
Totals	32	3	7	3	6	6

a-Popped out for Mirabelli in the 6th.

2B: Damon; HR: Ortiz, M. Ramirez 2; E: Timlin.

Red Sox	IP	H	R	ER	BB	SO
Wakefield (L)	5.1	6	4	4	1	4
Bradford	0.0	1	0	0	0	0
Myers	0.0	0	0	0	1	0
Papelbon	2.2	0	0	0	0	2
Timlin	1.0	1	1	1	0	1
Totals	9.0	8	5	5	2	7

HBP: Podsednik (by Wakefield), Everett (by Wakefield); T: 3:28; Att: 35,496.

Sox reliever Orlando Hernandez celebrates after striking out Red Sox Jason Varitek to end the eighth inning.
Photo by Tom Cruze/Sun-Times

me than for a guy that has been here one year. We've all been in this together from the get-go, and regardless of what [the celebration] looks like in here, we've always had our eyes on the big prize and we still do."

Only a week earlier, it was all but decided that Hernandez would not be helping the Sox toward that bigger prize—at least not in the Division Series. But two solid relief appearances against the Cleveland Indians convinced manager Ozzie Guillen and general manager Ken Williams to bring him along and let rookie Brandon McCarthy wait for a possible opportunity in the ALCS.

Playoff experience always has been the appeal with Hernandez, and he had another big-time per-

formance in a big game. He was called on in the sixth inning after Manny Ramirez brought the Red Sox within a run with his second homer and a shaky Damaso Marte loaded the bases with no one out on a single and two walks.

Hernandez's first bit of magic came when he retired pinch hitter Jason Varitek on a pop foul to Konerko. That was followed by a 10-pitch battle with Tony Graffanino that ended with a pop-up to shortstop Juan Uribe.

With Johnny Damon at the plate, Hernandez worked the count full, giving up ball three on a borderline pitch. He then retired the Red Sox' leadoff hitter on a check-swing strikeout to let a collective gasp of exasperation out of the crowd of 35,496.

But Hernandez wasn't finished. He pitched two more scoreless innings to get the White Sox to the ninth inning, where they were able to add an insurance run on a suicide squeeze by Uribe.

"He has [guts] and he has heart—that's established," pitching coach Don Cooper said. "He floated up on the shore of Miami [when he defected from Cuba]. He didn't take a plane or a boat; he floated. So the [guts] and heart are there.

"So this [game] out there … it's nothing to him. He is able to calm himself and execute the task at hand, which is making individual pitches, and you saw what he did. We needed somebody to step up in a big moment. Our backs were to the wall there a little bit. It was just wonderful to see what he did."

Bobby Jenks closed out the victory by getting Graffanino on a ground ball to third base, striking out Damon and ending it on Edgar Renteria's ground out to second base.

It set off an on-field celebration that dwarfed the modest show of emotion the Sox had when they clinched the division in Detroit.

"We knew we had a good group when everybody got together in spring training, but you don't know what you really have until you get out there and start battling," Scott Podsednik said. "But this team is resilient. To take two at home and to come to Fenway and to do what we've done, I'm hoping we can gain more confidence and take it into the next series."

Freddy Garcia, who won both the division clincher in Detroit and the ALDS clincher, got it done without his best stuff. He lasted only five-plus innings and gave up two home runs to Manny Ramirez and one to David Ortiz. But all three were

Orlando Hernandez leaps into closer Bobby Jenks's arms as the rest of the team rushes the field after they swept the Red Sox in the ALDS. Photo by Tom Cruze/Sun-Times

Sox manager Ozzie Guillen hugs Paul Konerko during the postgame celebration. Konerko's two-run homer in the sixth proved to be enough for the win. Photo by Tom Cruze/Sun-Times

solo shots, and Garcia was determined not to let anybody else beat him.

"I had seven days to pitch and I was feeling really good," Garcia said. "But I got out of situations a couple of times with double plays and gave up three solo home runs. It's great to beat those guys. You beat the champions. We weren't supposed to be here, and now we're celebrating."

Manager Ozzie Guillen guided the Sox to their first postseason series victory since the 1917 World Series, but he wasn't getting too caught up in the celebration.

"Every day it's somebody different on this team," Guillen said. "I'm so proud of the players because they just go there to bust their tails for all the fans and everyone in Chicago. They do a tremendous job and they never panic. That's why we are where we are."

—Written by Doug Padilla

AMERICAN LEAGUE CHAMPIONSHIP SERIES

ANGELS BEAT JETLAG

ANGELS 3, WHITE SOX 2
OCTOBER 11, 2005
U.S. CELLULAR FIELD

Jet lag trumped downtime as the road-weary Los Angeles Angels got a jump on the well-rested White Sox in the opener of the American League Championship Series.

Despite back-to-back overnight flights and some 5,000 air miles in the two days before the ALCS started, the Angels were fresh enough to get the best of the Sox' hottest starter in a 3-2 victory. The Sox will head into Game 2 down 1-0 in the series knowing that a failure to do the little things in the opener ended in their undoing.

"We just didn't execute very well tonight," said A.J. Pierzynski, who blundered when he thought he saw a sign for a hit and run in the seventh and was caught stealing. "We had a couple of chances to get a couple of bunts down and they got their bunt down and we didn't. In tight games like that, with the way the pitching is going, it ends up being a big thing."

The defeat snapped the Sox' three-game win streak in the postseason and their eight-game win streak including the regular season.

	1	2	3	4	5	6	7	8	9	R	H	E
Angels	0	1	2	0	0	0	0	0	0	3	7	1
White Sox	0	0	1	1	0	0	0	0	0	2	7	0

Angels	AB	R	H	RBI	BB	SO
Figgins, 3B	3	0	1	0	0	1
Cabrera, SS	4	0	1	1	0	0
Guerrero, DH	4	0	0	1	0	0
Anderson, LF	4	1	1	1	0	1
B. Molina, C	4	0	1	0	0	0
Erstad, 1B	4	0	1	0	0	0
Rivera, RF	4	0	0	0	0	0
Finley, CF	3	1	1	0	0	2
Kennedy, 2B	3	1	1	0	0	0
Totals	33	3	7	3	0	4

HR: Anderson; SB:Figgins, Erstad; E: Figgins.

Angels	IP	H	R	ER	BB	SO
Byrd (W)	6.0	5	2	2	1	1
Shields	2.0	2	0	0	0	1
Rodriguez (S)	1.0	0	0	0	0	1
Totals	9.0	7	2	2	1	3

White Sox	AB	R	H	RBI	BB	SO
Podsednik, LF	3	0	1	0	1	1
Iguchi, 2B	4	0	1	0	0	0
Dye, RF	4	0	1	0	0	0
Konerko, 1B	4	0	0	0	0	0
Everett, DH	4	1	1	0	0	0
Ozuna, PR-DH	0	0	0	0	0	0
Rowand, CF	3	0	0	0	0	0
Pierzynski, C	4	0	1	1	0	0
Crede, 3B	4	1	1	1	0	2
Uribe, SS	3	0	1	0	1	0
Totals	33	2	7	2	1	3

HR: Crede.

White Sox	IP	H	R	ER	BB	SO
Contreras (L)	8.1	7	3	3	0	4
Cotts	0.2	0	0	0	0	0
Totals	9.0	7	3	3	0	4

HBP: Rowand (by Byrd); T: 2:47; Att: 40,659.

Aaron Rowand tumbles backward in the seventh inning as he is forced out at second base on a fielder's choice to Angels short-stop Orlando Cabrera. Photo by Tom Cruze/Sun-Times

For Jose Contreras, it was his first defeat since falling to the Minnesota Twins on Aug. 15. He closed the season by winning his final eight starts and added a ninth in Game 1 of the AL Division Series against the Boston Red Sox.

Contreras pitched well enough to win, but the Angels were able to cash in just enough opportunities and received a clutch outing from starter Paul Byrd. The Sox' right-hander arguably delivered the better outing but ended up with nothing to show for it.

After giving up a leadoff home run on a 2-0 pitch to Garret Anderson to open the second inning, Contreras had just enough hard luck in the third to fall into a 3-0 hole.

"When you lose it's always a bad outing regardless of how you pitch or how many strike-outs you had or what you threw," Contreras said through interpreter Ozzie Guillen Jr. "The problem came with falling behind on Garret Anderson. Falling behind such a good hitter, you have to attack him, and if you attack him the wrong way, you're going to get hurt."

Steve Finley and Adam Kennedy led off the third inning with singles and were moved over on a bunt from Chone Figgins. Finley scored when Joe Crede was unable to make a play on a slow roller to third by Orlando Cabrera, and Kennedy scored when Tadahito Iguchi failed to complete a 1-4-3 double play to end the inning. Instead of going

Scott Podsednik pops out in the first inning. Podsednik had a hit, struck out and walked once. Photo by Jon Sall/Sun-Times

home on a comebacker, Contreras threw to Iguchi, who appeared to anticipate a hard slide from Cabrera and threw over Paul Konerko's head at first base.

Byrd likely would not have even been on the mound for the Angels had Bartolo Colon not injured his shoulder early in the ALDS series-clinching victory over the New York Yankees.

How fitting that Byrd was unaffected by so much flying. ... The right-hander gave up just two runs on five hits in six-plus innings, getting pulled after just 73 pitches. With the Sox trailing 3-0 in the third inning, Byrd gave up his first run on a solo home run to Crede, his first of the postseason. Crede entered having collected just one hit in nine at-bats in the ALDS.

The Sox cut the lead to 3-2 in the fourth on a two-out RBI single from Pierzynski. From then on, the Sox failed to make things happen like they seemed to do so easily in the sweep over the Red Sox.

In the fifth inning, Scott Podsednik received a one-out walk, but was thrown out trying to steal

Sox manager Ozzie Guillen pulls starter Jose Contreras in the top of the ninth inning. Photo by Jon Sall/Sun-Times

on a pitchout. To start the sixth inning, No. 3 hitter Jermaine Dye popped up a bunt.

The seventh inning was another wasted opportunity. Aaron Rowand was hit by Byrd on the first pitch of the inning, convincing Angels manager Mike Scioscia to make a pitching change. After Scot Shields got Pierzynski to hit into a force out, Crede took a pitch and Pierzynski easily was caught stealing.

"I saw hit and run so I took off," Pierzynski said. "Did I miss a sign? I guess I did, I don't know. I asked [first-base coach Tim Raines], and he wasn't sure, either."

In the eighth, Juan Uribe and Dye came through with singles, but Konerko popped out to center to end the threat. The final lost opportunity came in the ninth. Carl Everett reached base on a Figgins error, but Rowand failed to get down a sacrifice bunt.

"This wasn't our best game execution-wise, which isn't good," Konerko said. "I think a positive we can take out of it is that I didn't think we played well at all but we lost by a run. I feel if we shore up those things and tighten up our game, then it will be better for us. That's what we do. That's why we're here. We've been successful doing that all year, and so have they. They were just better at it."

—Written by Doug Padilla

SOXRUNANDSTUN

WHITE SOX 2, ANGELS 1
OCTOBER 12, 2005
U.S. CELLULAR FIELD

The perceived short hop that put a spring into the step of the White Sox is likely to be debated for some time.

With the White Sox struggling to put together any kind of offensive attack, A.J. Pierzynski created his own rally on a strikeout of all things, and Joe Crede did the rest with a game-winning double in the bottom of the ninth to give the Sox a 2-1 victory and a 1-1 tie in the American League Championship Series.

The pesky Pierzynski, who never met an opponent that appreciated his act, made himself a menace to the opposite side once again. After he appeared to strike out on a low fastball from Kelvim Escobar to send the game into extra innings, Pierzynski broke for first base as Angels catcher Josh Paul rolled the ball back to the mound.

While home-plate umpire Doug Eddings appeared to signal that Pierzynski was out, he said afterward that was only his "mechanic" for a swing-

		1	2	3	4	5	6	7	8	9	R	H	E
Angels		0	0	0	0	1	0	0	0	0	1	5	3
White Sox		1	0	0	0	0	0	0	0	1	2	7	1

Angels	AB	R	H	RBI	BB	SO
Figgins, CF	4	0	0	0	0	0
Cabrera, SS	4	0	2	0	0	0
Guerrero, RF	4	0	0	0	0	0
B. Molina, DH	3	0	0	0	0	1
Anderson, LF	4	0	0	0	0	1
Quinlan, 3B	3	1	1	1	0	2
Erstad, 1B	3	0	1	0	0	0
J. Molina, C	3	0	1	0	0	0
DaVanon, PR	0	0	0	0	0	0
Paul, C	0	0	0	0	0	0
Kennedy, 2B	2	0	0	0	0	0
Totals	30	1	5	1	0	4

2B: Cabrera; HR: Quinlan; E: Washburn, Guerrero, Paul

Angels	IP	H	R	ER	BB	SO
Washburn	4.2	4	1	0	1	1
Donnelly	0.1	0	0	0	0	1
Shields	1.0	0	0	0	0	2
Escobar (L)	2.2	3	1	0	0	5
Totals	9.0	7	2	0	1	9

White Sox	AB	R	H	RBI	BB	SO
Podsednik, LF	4	1	1	0	0	1
Iguchi, 2B	2	0	0	0	0	1
Dye, RF	4	0	1	1	0	1
Konerko, 1B	4	0	1	0	0	2
Everett, DH	4	0	0	0	0	1
Rowand, CF	4	0	1	0	0	1
Pierzynski, C	3	0	0	0	1	2
Ozuna, PR	0	1	0	0	0	0
Crede, 3B	4	0	2	1	0	0
Uribe, SS	3	0	1	0	0	0
Totals	32	2	7	2	1	9

2B: Rowand, Crede 2; SB: Ozuna; E: Uribe.

White Sox	IP	H	R	ER	BB	SO
Buehrle (W)	9.0	5	1	1	0	4
Totals	9.0	5	1	1	0	4

HBP: Iguchi (by Washburn), B. Molina (by Buehrle); T: 2:34; Att: 41,013.

A.J. Pierzynski heads to first base after striking out in the ninth. Angels catcher Josh Paul did not tag him or throw to first and Pierzynski was awarded the base. Photo by Tom Cruze/Sun-Times

ing third strike and the play still was live. Pierzynski reached first base with ease, and the Angels cried foul. Manager Mike Scioscia argued with Eddings to no avail, and television replays show Paul, a former member of the White Sox, trapped the ball near the ground with a backhand attempt.

THE RULE

Rule 6.09 (b): The batter becomes a runner when the third strike called by the umpire is not caught, providing (1) first base is unoccupied, or (2) first base is occupied with two out; when a batter becomes a baserunner on a third strike not caught by the catcher and starts for the dugout, or his position, and then realizes his situation and attempts then to reach first base, he is not out unless he or first base is tagged before he reaches first base. *Source: Official rules of Major League Baseball*

"You're taught that if the third strike is in the dirt you run, and Josh didn't tag me," Pierzynski said. "I think he thought he caught it. I just ran, and luckily it worked out."

Eddings, crew chief Jerry Crawford and umpire supervisor Rich Reiker all were available afterward to explain their view of the play.

Pinch-running for A.J. Pierzynski, Pablo Ozuna scores the winning run on a hit by Joe Crede in the ninth.
Photo by Tom Cruze/Sun-Times

"We have some [replay] technology, and Jerry Crawford saw it, also the whole crew, and there was definitely a change in [ball] direction there," Reiker said. "At this point, I would say at best it's inconclusive. I wouldn't totally agree that the ball was caught, but there was a change in direction there that we saw and the replay is available to us."

Pablo Ozuna replaced Pierzynski at first base, and the Sox took full advantage of their second chance. Ozuna stole second base without a throw, and Crede followed with a line drive off the wall in left for the game-winner. What added to the Angels' pain is that Crede's shot came on an 0-2 pitch.

"He threw a [split-finger pitch] right there, and it kind of hung up in the zone," Crede said. "He had a good splitter working tonight, and it just didn't drop off the table like he wanted it to."

The run made a winner out of Mark Buehrle, who had just one blemish in this outing, when Robb Quinlan led off the fifth inning with a home run to tie the score 1-1. Buehrle went nine innings in just his second career postseason start.

Buehrle gave up five hits in the complete game and was never in serious danger other than the Quinlan home run and a fly ball to the wall by Orlando Cabrera to end the top of the eighth inning with a runner on base. It was the fourth time Buehrle has pitched a complete game this season, and over his last three starts (23-2/3 innings) the left-hander has given up just 12 hits and two earned runs for a 0.76 ERA.

"It was probably one of the best games of my career," Buehrle said. "We found my changeup in the middle innings, and in the seventh and eighth innings I made a couple of key pitches and had a

The White Sox celebrate at the plate after pinch runner Pablo Ozuna scored the winning run. Photo by Tom Cruze/Sun-Times

ground ball and a couple of outs. But it was one of the best games of my career."

How big was this victory? Considering that the Sox were close to falling behind 2-0 in the series and that five of the last six teams to win Game 2 have gone on to win the ALCS, nobody was fretting over an offense that appears to have gone stagnant again.

"Well, we don't have good swings, that's all," manager Ozzie Guillen said. "You don't get here with a bad pitching staff. They have a good pitching staff. I think they have one of the best bullpens in baseball, the kind you don't want to play. I think you have to give them credit. When you go to the bullpen, you're going to have a tough time scoring runs."

The Sox appeared to be off and running in the first inning by catching the kind of break that didn't materialize in Game 1. Scott Podsednik hit a comebacker to Angels starter Jarrod Washburn to open the game, and the left-hander lobbed the ball over the head of first baseman Darin Erstad to allow Podsednik to advance to second base.

Tadahito Iguchi followed with a sacrifice bunt to move Podsednik to third base, and Jermaine Dye gave the Sox a 1-0 lead on a ground ball to shortstop.

"This is two really good teams battling each other, and every pitch counts," Pierzynski said. "It's fun to be out there to see the games, and it's amazing how much rides on every pitch in this series. So far, the first two games have lived up to every expectation, and hopefully it can keep going."

—Written by Doug Padilla

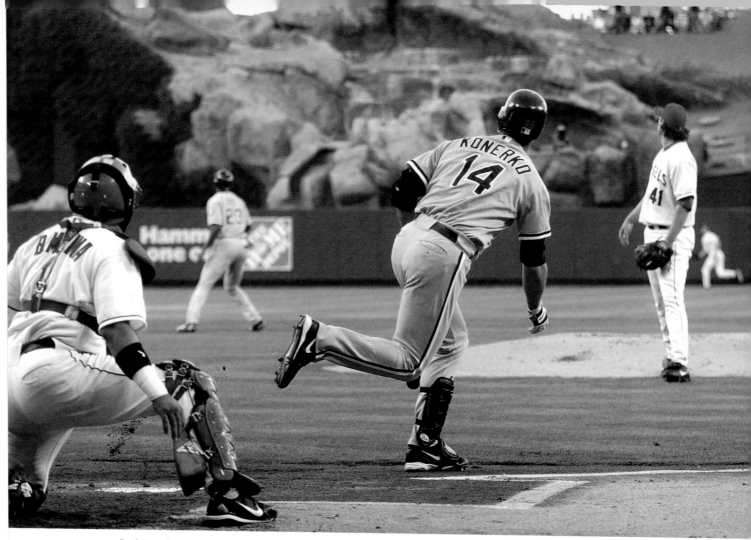

Paul Konerko starts around the bases while the Angels watch his two-run homer sail out of the park. Photo by Tom Cruze/Sun-Times

"It was big," manager Ozzie Guillen said of the first-inning production. "I think Lackey is one of the best pitchers they have. I think the first inning set the tone. We didn't know how Garland would show up because of the layoff. I was worried about it. But when we scored in the first inning, every time we score in the first inning, it seems like we play better baseball. That first inning set the tone, and we played the game we always play."

Garland got off to just the start he needed, considering he hadn't pitched in two weeks. He walked Chone Figgins on seven pitches to lead off the game but got Orlando Cabrera to strike out and Vladimir Guerrero to hit into a double play to end the first inning. With two outs in the fourth, Garland had faced the minimum 11 batters until a Guerrero infield single that glanced off the pitcher's right foot.

"It's something they have been doing all year that got them to this point," Angels manager Mike Scioscia said. "It's incredible starting pitching. I think if you look at Jon Garland's chart, I'd be surprised if he missed with a dozen pitches in spots. That might have been one of the top couple of games pitched against us all year.

"Coming off the heels of what Buehrle did the other night and [Jose] Contreras in Game 1, those horses they have up front—especially if you give them the lead—they can pitch deep into a game."

The Sox had pushed their lead to 4-0 on a bloop single to left by Carl Everett in the third inning, and in the fifth they made it 5-0 when Konerko belted a two-out single to center to score Iguchi, who had doubled.

Garland was cruising until an Adam Kennedy single with one out in the sixth. With two outs,

Third baseman Joe Crede lays the tag on Darin Erstad as he tries to stretch a double into a triple for the third out of the second inning. Photo by Tom Cruze/Sun-Times

Cabrera homered to left and cut the lead to 5-2. Not letting the home run affect him, Garland retired the last 10 batters of the game. He gave up just four hits and had seven strikeouts, allowing only the Figgins walk.

"A.J. came out and calmed me down [after the home run]," said Garland, who stayed away from his sinker and dominated with a four-seam fastball that he often delivered in on the hands. "I was upset with the pitch I threw. I was mad at myself because I shook him, and he wanted something different. But he was able to come out and calm me down, two outs, jump back on the mound, and here we go."

The two complete games, along with Contreras's 8-1/3 innings in the opener, means the Sox bullpen has been used for just two-thirds of an inning in the series. Only left-hander Neal Cotts has seen action in relief against the Angels.

And to think, just a few seasons ago Garland nearly was traded to the Angels for a package that would have netted the Sox Darin Erstad. An executive for Disney, which owned the team at the time, thought Garland wasn't a marketable enough name. But he was as good as they come in this outing.

"It happens all the time in baseball these days, trades, moving around," Garland said. "It happened to me in '98 as a young kid getting traded to the White Sox. It's business. You've got to understand that.

"If it would have happened, it would have happened, and I would have made the best of it."

—Written by Doug Padilla

SOXMOVEONE STEPCLOSER

WHITE SOX 8, ANGELS 2
OCTOBER 15, 2005
ANGEL STADIUM AT ANAHEIM

The White Sox' march to the World Series has become so methodical, so precise, so matter-of-fact that all the drama of a franchise changing the course of its history has been lost thus far.

The American League Championship Series has featured nothing like the hypertension last season that saw the Boston Red Sox overcome a 3-0 deficit against the New York Yankees in the ALCS, then mow down the St. Louis Cardinals in the World Series.

The Sox are scoring early, watching their starters dominate and leaving the theatrics under wraps. Even general manager Ken Williams, who typically is high-strung when watching games, has been in need of a little pick-me-up. In the seventh inning of the Sox' 8-2 victory against the Los Angeles Angels in Game 4 of the ALCS, Williams was chatting it up with comedian George Lopez in his private box.

Despite the Sox' solid play and a 3-1 ALCS lead, nobody is forgetting that the Yankees were in even

	1	2	3	4	5	6	7	8	9	R	H	E
White Sox	3	0	1	1	1	0	0	2	0	8	8	1
Angels	0	1	0	1	0	0	0	0	0	2	6	1

White Sox	AB	R	H	RBI	BB	SO
Podsednik, LF	2	2	1	0	3	0
Iguchi, 2B	4	1	0	0	0	2
Dye, RF	5	1	0	0	0	0
Konerko, 1B	4	1	1	3	1	0
Everett, DH	3	1	2	2	1	0
Rowand, CF	4	1	1	0	0	1
Pierzynski, C	4	1	1	1	0	2
Crede, 3B	4	0	2	2	0	1
Uribe, SS	3	0	0	0	1	0
Totals	33	8	8	8	6	6

2B: Rowand; 3B: Podsednik; HR: Konerko, Pierzynski;
SB: Dye, Podsednik 2; E: Garcia

White Sox	IP	H	R	ER	BB	SO
Garcia (W)	9.0	6	2	2	1	5
Totals	9.0	6	2	2	1	5

Angels	AB	R	H	RBI	BB	SO
Figgins, 3B	4	0	0	0	0	2
Cabrera, SS	4	0	0	0	0	0
Izturis, SS	0	0	0	0	0	0
Guerrero, RF	4	0	0	0	0	0
Anderson, LF	4	1	1	0	0	2
Erstad, 1B	3	1	1	0	0	0
DaVanon, PR	0	0	0	0	0	0
Kotchman, DH	4	0	2	1	0	0
B. Molina, C	3	0	1	1	0	0
Finley, CF	3	0	1	0	0	0
Kennedy, 2B	3	0	0	0	0	1
Totals	32	2	6	2	1	5

2B: Kotchman; E: Cabrera.

Angels	IP	H	R	ER	BB	SO
Santana (L)	4.1	3	6	5	3	2
Shields	1.2	2	0	0	1	1
Donnelly	1.0	0	0	0	1	1
Yan	2.0	3	2	2	1	2
Totals	9.0	8	8	7	6	6

HBP: Iguchi (By Santana); T: 2.46; Att: 44,857.

Angels first baseman Darin Erstad leaps to corral a high throw by shortstop Orlando Cabrera. Jermaine Dye was ruled safe on the play and later scored. Photo by Tom Cruze/Sun-Times

Starter Freddy Garcia delivers to the plate. Garcia pitched a complete game for the Sox. Photo by Tom Cruze/Sun-Times

better shape last season as they moved a game away from the World Series. They came up empty-handed.

"We are not the type of team that is cocky," manager Ozzie Guillen said. "The cockiest guy on that team is me, and I'm pretty low-key in the play-offs. I always tell my guys that no matter what happens tonight, it doesn't mean anything tomorrow. When you play a short series, anything can happen. We're playing our kind of game, but with the kind of ballclub [the Angels] have, they can turn it around. Anything can happen."

The big blow came early for the second consecutive game, with Paul Konerko delivering a three-run home run in the first inning to start the Sox on their way. With every run-producing swing from the soon-to-be free agent, Konerko's offseason price tag seems to rise. He has two homers and six RBI in the first four games of the ALCS and four homers and 10 RBI in the playoffs.

"To watch Paul do what he's done this series has been ... well, the guy has just been fun to watch," said leadoff man Scott Podsednik, who reached base four times and scored two runs. "We like our chances with guys on base and him at the plate."

Konerko's effort has put the Sox one victory from their first World Series appearance since 1959 and five victories from their first World Series title since 1917. And in a sign that the Sox are oblivious to demons young and old, they are delivering on the West Coast, where recent visits have been humbling.

With pitching like the Sox are getting in the postseason, it is no wonder opponents are falling by the wayside. Freddy Garcia delivered the fourth consecutive strong outing for the Sox and did so after a seven-day rest that included the birth of his first child.

"They're getting strike one, they're getting ahead and all of them have been able to use all of their pitches in any situation," catcher A.J. Pierzynski said about the common thread among Sox starters. "They have been able to throw curve, slider, changeup, fastball. They've all been able to

Sox third baseman Joe Crede dives to stop a drive by Vladimir Guerrero in the sixth inning. Crede found his feet and threw Guerrero out. Photo by Tom Cruze/Sun-Times

do it. But the key is they get ahead, and once we get ahead they've been pretty good at putting guys away."

Garcia's complete game was the third in a row for the Sox, who apparently brought along their relievers just so there wouldn't be too many empty lockers in the clubhouse and there would be more hands available to spray champagne. It is the first time a team has delivered three consecutive complete games in the postseason since the New York Mets' Tom Seaver, Jon Matlack and Jerry Koosman did it in the 1973 National League Championship Series. But Seaver's was in defeat.

Garcia set up an Angels run with a throwing error in the second and gave up another on a double by Casey Kotchman in the fourth. Then he got downright stingy, retiring 16 of the last 18 batters.

When Darin Erstad singled with two outs in the ninth, Guillen came to the mound.

"I went out in the last inning and talked to Freddy to see if he had enough [because] I had a lefty ready," Guillen said. "Freddy gave me the right answer: 'You're not getting me out of here.' That meant he wanted to follow his teammates and what they did in the couple of days before."

The night certainly would not have been complete without another incident involving Pierzynski. When Steve Finley hit into an inning-ending double play with a runner on third in the second, his bat actually clipped Pierzynski's glove, which should have been catcher's interference. Instead of Finley being awarded first base, Garcia was out of his only real jam.

Pierzynski, who has been booed all series after his incident in the ninth inning of Game 2, made an impact again with a fourth-inning homer that gave the Sox a 5-1 lead.

—Written by Doug Padilla

SOX ARE GO-GO-GOING TO SERIES

WHITE SOX 6, ANGELS 3
OCTOBER 16, 2005
ANGEL STADIUM OF ANAHEIM

A White Sox team that has been compared all season to its predecessor of five decades ago now will head to where that team fell short.

The White Sox' previous World Series team in 1959 was known as the "Go-Go Sox," and this season there has been a revival on the South Side. Sure, the 2005 Sox have run, but mostly they pitched themselves into the Fall Classic with a 6-3 victory over the Los Angeles Angels.

While Nellie Fox, Ted Kluszewski and Luis Aparicio put an offensive charge into the '59 team,

the current Sox have been doing it with pitching from Jose Contreras, Mark Buehrle, Jon Garland and Freddy Garcia.

It was Contreras's turn to carry the Sox, and he found himself in a tight battle amid a steady mist that started falling just before game time. In the end, the light rain would be nothing compared to a third champagne shower in a little over two weeks as the Sox have now celebrated a Central Division title, an American League Division Series triumph and an AL Championship Series domination of the Angels.

	1	2	3	4	5	6	7	8	9	R	H	E
White Sox	0	1	0	0	1	0	1	1	2	6	8	1
Angels	0	0	1	0	2	0	0	0	0	3	5	2

White Sox	AB	R	H	RBI	BB	SO
Podsednik, LF	3	0	0	0	2	2
Iguchi, 2B	3	1	0	0	1	1
Dye, RF	4	1	2	1	1	1
Konerko, 1B	5	0	1	1	0	1
Everett, DH	5	0	1	0	0	2
Rowand, CF	3	2	1	1	1	0
Pierzynski, C	3	0	0	0	0	1
Crede, 3B	3	1	2	3	0	0
Uribe, SS	3	1	1	0	1	1
Totals	32	6	8	6	6	9

Angels	AB	R	H	RBI	BB	SO
Figgins, 3B	3	1	1	1	0	0
Cabrera, SS	4	0	0	0	0	0
Anderson, CF	2	0	1	1	1	0
Guerrero, RF	4	0	0	0	0	0
Erstad, 1B	4	0	0	0	0	1
B. Molina, C	4	0	0	0	0	0
Kotchman, DH	3	0	0	0	1	1
Rivera, LF	3	1	1	0	0	0
Kennedy, 2B	3	1	2	1	0	0
Totals	30	3	5	3	2	2

2B: Rowand, Uribe, Dye, Konerko; HR: Crede; SB: Podsednik; E: Contreras.

2B: Rivera, Figgins; E: Escobar, Kennedy.

White Sox	IP	H	R	ER	BB	SO
Contreras (W)	9.0	5	3	3	2	2
Totals	9.0	5	3	3	2	2

Angels	IP	H	R	ER	BB	SO
Byrd	4.2	5	2	2	1	1
Shields	1.1	0	0	0	0	1
Escobar (BS, L)	1.2	1	2	1	2	5
Rodriguez	1.1	2	2	0	3	2
Totals	9.0	8	6	3	6	9

HBP: Iguchi (by Byrd); T: 3:11; Att: 44,712.

Joe Crede laces a single up the middle in the eighth to score Aaron Rowand and put the Sox ahead 4-3. Photo by Tom Cruze/Sun-Times

Contreras finished with the Sox' fourth-consecutive complete game, an LCS record. It's the most consecutive complete games in the postseason since the 1956 New York Yankees got five in a row from Whitey Ford, Tom Sturdivant, Don Larsen (a perfect game), Bob Turley, and Johnny Kucks.

In the only real competition of note over the past week, a late debate raged over who would win the ALCS MVP, Joe Crede or Paul Konerko. An insurance RBI double in the ninth inning for Konerko gave him the edge as he finished the series with six hits, including two home runs, and seven RBI. Crede, who delivered a game-tying home run in the seventh inning and drove home the go-ahead run with a single in the eighth, had seven hits, including two home runs, and six RBI.

"You can split up [the MVP] about 10 different ways," Konerko said. "I mean, four complete games in a row, you have to be kidding me. But I know who the real MVP is, and that's our pitching. I'm still going to respect it, and I'll honor it, but it's all about team here."

Contreras gave up three runs and five hits with two walks and two strikeouts and threw 114 pitches.

"Believe it or not, you get ready for this game from Day One in spring training," Contreras said through interpreter Ozzie Guillen Jr. "That's what all the teams are out there to do, to pitch in the postseason and eventually go to the World Series.

"Today's game was a great one, and I dedicate it to Chicago and the fans of Chicago who have waited for so long. I know they deserve this because

Jermaine Dye and Paul Konerko meet Aaron Rowand at the dugout steps after he scored the go-ahead run on a Joe Crede hit in the eighth inning. Photo by Tom Cruze/Sun-Times

they stood by me when I was pitching bad and now that I'm pitching great."

Like they did in their previous three victories against the Angels, the Sox jumped out in front early, although they waited until the second inning to do it. Aaron Rowand doubled, was moved to third on a sacrifice bunt by A.J. Pierzynski and scored on a sacrifice fly from Joe Crede.

The Angels, though, would not go as easily. They tied the score 1-1 on an Adam Kennedy single in the third inning. Vladimir Guerrero had a chance to add to the scoring, but he failed to come through with runners on the corners and two outs. Guerrero, who grounded out, went 1-for-20 in the series.

The Sox grabbed the lead back in the fifth inning on a clutch two-out double from Jermaine Dye, but the Angels went on top 3-2 on a ground-

rule double from Chone Figgins and a sacrifice fly from Garret Anderson.

It was then Crede's turn to shine. Against Kelvim Escobar to open the seventh inning, Crede tied the score 3-3 on a home run to left field off an 0-1 pitch.

Things got wacky in the eighth inning, and, of course, Pierzynski was right in the middle of it. After Konerko and Carl Everett struck out to open the inning, Rowand walked. Pierzynski hit a dribbler down the first-base line that Escobar fielded, but he inexplicably tagged Pierzynski with his glove as the ball was in his bare hand.

First-base umpire Randy Marsh initially called Pierzynski out, and Guillen immediately sprinted from the dugout to argue.

The umpires met near the mound and reversed the call. Closer Francisco Rodriguez was called

Sox owner Jerry Reinsdorf shares the American League Championship trophy with manager Ozzie Guillen during the postgame celebration. Photo by Tom Cruze/Sun-Times

from the bullpen to face Crede, and after just missing the strike zone on 1-2 and 2-2 pitches, Crede sent a full-count bouncer over the mound toward center field. Second baseman Kennedy dove to stop the ball on the grass in shallow center field, but his rainbow throw to the plate to cut down a diving Rowand was not in time, and the Sox went up 4-3.

"That's the thing about this game, to be in the right place at the right time," Crede said. "I was fortunate to be in this situation where I could do something to help us win. I was able to put enough good wood on the ball and put it in play and get a hit out of it."

Contreras closed out the victory in the ninth by getting Erstad on a bouncer to shortstop for the first out and Molina on a fly ball to center for out No. 2. When Konerko fielded a Casey Kotchman

ground ball and stepped on first base, the celebration was on.

"We still have some work to do," a champagne-soaked chairman Jerry Reinsdorf said in the clubhouse afterward. "We still have to get four more wins. It feels wonderful, but there still is a lot more work to be done.

"No matter what happens, when you win the American League pennant, you've had one wonderful year. But then you get greedy, and you want to get four more. It's only been since 1917, so I think it's time, and hopefully these guys can get the job done."

—Written by Doug Padilla

JOE, PEN AND SHUT

WHITE SOX 5, ASTROS 3
OCTOBER 22, 2005
U.S. CELLULAR FIELD

The Sox won the opener of the World Series by a hair, or so it seemed with shaggy Joe Crede leading the way.

Like his untamed mane, Crede was all over the place with his bat and glove in Game 1 as he helped clean up on the Houston Astros in a 5-3 victory. The hair that stuck out from under his helmet flapped in the breeze as he rounded the bases after a fourth-inning go-ahead home run, and he nearly dirtied his trendy goatee a couple of times by hitting the dirt to take away a pair of potential RBI doubles.

There was some symmetry in the Sox winning a World Series game started by future Hall of Famer Roger Clemens. Their last World Series victory came Oct. 6, 1959, in a game started by Los Angeles Dodgers Hall of Famer Sandy Koufax. The Sox have now won five consecutive playoff games and 13 of their last 14 games dating back to the regular season.

After just missing out on American League Championship Series MVP honors—he delivered two game-winning hits—Crede showed he still had plenty in reserve for an even bigger stage.

	1	2	3	4	5	6	7	8	9	R	H	E
Astros	0	1	2	0	0	0	0	0	0	3	7	1
White Sox	1	2	0	1	0	0	0	1	X	5	10	0

Astros	AB	R	H	RBI	BB	SO
Biggio, 2B	4	1	1	0	0	0
Taveras, CF	3	0	2	0	0	0
Berkman, LF	4	0	2	2	0	1
Burke, PR-LF	0	0	0	0	0	0
Ensberg, 3B	4	0	0	0	0	1
Lamb, 1B	4	1	1	1	0	2
Bagwell, DH	2	0	0	0	0	1
Lane, RF	4	0	0	0	0	1
Ausmus, C	3	0	1	0	0	0
Everett, SS	4	1	0	0	0	1
Totals	32	3	7	3	0	7

White Sox	AB	R	H	RBI	BB	SO
Podsednik, LF	5	0	2	1	0	1
Iguchi, 2B	5	0	0	0	0	1
Dye, RF	2	1	1	1	2	0
Konerko, 1B	4	0	2	0	0	0
Everett, DH	3	1	1	0	0	1
Rowand, CF	3	0	1	0	1	1
Pierzynski, C	4	2	1	1	0	0
Crede, 3B	4	1	1	1	0	0
Uribe, SS	2	0	1	1	2	0
Totals	32	5	10	5	5	4

2B: Berkman, Taveras 2; HR: Lamb; SB: Burke; E: Everett.

2B: Uribe; 3B: Podsednik; HR: Dye, Crede; SB: Podsednik, Pierzynski.

Astros	IP	H	R	ER	BB	SO
Clemens	2.0	4	3	3	0	1
Rodriguez (L)	3.1	4	1	1	5	1
Qualls	1.2	0	0	0	0	2
Springer	1.0	2	1	1	0	0
Totals	8.0	10	5	5	5	4

White Sox	IP	H	R	ER	BB	SO
Contreras (W)	7.0	6	3	3	0	2
Cotts	0.2	1	0	0	0	2
Jenks (S)	1.1	0	0	0	0	3
Totals	9.0	7	3	3	0	7

HBP: Bagwell (by Contreras), Bagwell (by Contreras), Ausmus (by Contreras); T: 3:13; Att: 41,206.

Joe Crede launches a solo homer in the fourth inning to put the Sox up 4-3. Photo by Tom Cruze/Sun-Times

With Clemens gone after two innings because of a strained left hamstring, Crede broke a 3-3 tie in the fourth with his solo home run off reliever Wandy Rodriguez.

"That's the Joe we expected," manager Ozzie Guillen said. "I think this kid really had a tough year. We expected a lot from him, and all of a sudden he started swinging the bat real good at the right moments. We were really struggling when he came back [Sept. 10] from the [disabled list]. He had a broken finger for a little while, and all of a sudden he [came back] and started swinging the bat good, and he helped this team to be where we are."

Crede also won the last playoff game at U.S. Cellular Field on Oct. 12, when he connected on a double off the left-field wall in the ninth inning, one batter after A.J. Pierzynski reached first on the strikeout heard 'round the baseball world. And he worked his heroics in the ALCS clincher when his home run in the seventh inning of Game 5 against the Los Angeles Angels tied the score and his single in the eighth gave the Sox the go-ahead run.

Before the bullpen came on to bail out Jose Contreras in the eighth inning, Crede was there with his glove in the sixth and seventh. With Willy Taveras on third base in the sixth with one out and the infield in, Crede reached across his body and went to the ground to stab a hard-hit ball from Morgan Ensberg. He got to his feet and threw across the infield for the second out. Contreras

Closer Bobby Jenks celebrates after earning the save against the Astros. Photo by Tom Cruze/Sun-Times

ended the threat by retiring Mike Lamb on a grounder to second.

In the seventh, Contreras was in even more hot water. After Contreras hit two batters, and with runners on first and third with two outs, Crede again reached across his body, diving to stop a ground ball down the line by Craig Biggio to end the inning.

It was a rusty bullpen's turn to play savior in the eighth. Neal Cotts, who last pitched in Game 1 of the ALCS, replaced Contreras after Taveras led off with a double. Lance Berkman's single to left was hit too hard for Taveras to score, but the Astros had runners on the corners and nobody out.

Cotts struck out Ensberg and Lamb before turning things over to Bobby Jenks.

The big right-hander, who hadn't pitched in 15 days, turned up the heat on designated hitter Jeff Bagwell, starting his first game since May 3. Jenks got ahead on the count 0-2 on two 99 mph fastballs before cranking it up to 100 on his next three pitches. The third fastball in triple digits got Bagwell swinging.

"I thought we had a chance against Cotts; we had some chances," Astros manager Phil Garner said. "They strike out Morgan, who is a good hitter, and they strike out Lamb who is a good hitter. That ended up being the ballgame."

Sox third base coach Joey Cora congratulates Jermaine Dye after his solo home run in the first inning.
Photo by Tom Cruze/Sun-Times

Jenks recorded the final three outs in the ninth for the save.

The Sox started early on a shaky Clemens. Jermaine Dye delivered a two-out homer in the first on a full count after a nine-pitch battle. The shot to right was the Sox' first home run in a World Series game since Ted Kluszewski hit one in Game 6 in 1959.

Contreras, who won 11 games in the second half, looked shaky in the third inning when he gave up two runs on a two-out double to Berkman to tie the score 3-3. Crede's homer off Rodriguez put the Sox on top for good.

Clemens said his hamstring caused trouble in the second, "and I fought my way through that inning. I came [to the clubhouse] as quick as I could to take my sleeve off and have them check to see if there was anything I could do so I could continue. The fluid already started to build up in my leg."

The Sox wasted a prime scoring opportunity in the fifth, failing to produce with the bases loaded and one out. An insurance run finally came in the eighth as Scott Podsednik delivered a two-out RBI triple against reliever Russ Springer.

—Written by Doug Padilla

Starting pitcher Jose Contreras delivers to an Astros batter early in Game 1 of the World Series. Photo by Jon Sall/Sun-Times

First baseman Paul Konerko makes the catch on a Jason Lane foul in the seventh. Photo by Jon Sall/Sun-Times

JENKSOFF SCOTTFREE

WHITE SOX 7, ASTROS 6
OCTOBER 23, 2005
U.S. CELLULAR FIELD

The high drama that had been missing from much of the White Sox' championship run came in a deluge as Paul Konerko looked to be the hero, Bobby Jenks looked to be the goat and light-hitting Scott Podsednik muscled up while riding to the rescue.

Without a home run all season, Podsednik now has two in the postseason and none bigger than his shot to right-center field with one out in

the ninth inning off Houston Astros' All-Star closer Brad Lidge to give the Sox a 7-6 victory and a 2-0 lead in the World Series. It was the 14th walk-off home run in World Series history and helped take the misery out of a chilly, rain-soaked night.

"I was just trying to get on base, then we can work from there, then we'll try to get into scoring position," Podsednik said. "Luckily, I got [the count] to 2-1, and I said, 'Hey, let's put a good

	1	2	3	4	5	6	7	8	9	R	H	E
Astros	0	1	1	0	2	0	0	0	2	6	9	0
White Sox	0	2	0	0	0	0	4	0	1	7	12	0

Astros	AB	R	H	RBI	BB	SO
Biggio, 2B	4	0	0	0	0	1
Bruntlett, 2B	0	0	0	0	0	0
b-Lamb, PH-1B	1	0	0	0	0	0
Taveras, CF	4	2	2	0	0	0
Berkman, 1B-LF	3	0	1	3	0	2
Ensberg, 3B	4	1	1	1	0	1
Bagwell, DH	4	1	1	0	0	0
Lane, RF	4	0	1	0	0	2
Burke, LF-2B	3	1	0	0	1	0
Ausmus, C	4	1	2	0	0	0
Everett, SS	3	0	0	0	0	2
a-Vizcaino, PH-SS	1	0	1	2	0	0
Totals	35	6	9	6	1	8

a-Singled for Everett in the 9th. b-Flied out for Bruntlett in the 9th.

2B: Ausmus, Berkman; 3B: Taveras; HR: Ensberg; SB: Lane.

Astros	IP	H	R	ER	BB	SO
Pettitte	6.0	8	2	2	0	4
Wheeler	0.2	1	3	3	1	1
Qualls (BS)	0.2	2	1	1	0	0
Gallo	0.2	0	0	0	0	0
Lidge (L)	0.1	1	1	1	0	0
Totals	8.1	12	7	7	1	5

White Sox	AB	R	H	RBI	BB	SO
Podsednik, LF	5	1	1	1	0	1
Iguchi, 2B	3	1	1	0	1	1
Dye, RF	3	1	1	0	0	0
Konerko, 1B	4	1	1	4	0	1
Everett, DH	4	0	2	0	0	1
Rowand, CF	4	1	2	0	0	0
Pierzynski, C	4	1	1	0	0	1
Crede, 3B	4	0	1	1	0	0
Uribe, SS	4	1	2	1	0	0
Totals	35	7	12	7	1	5

2B: Uribe 2, Rowand; HR: Konerko, Podsednik; SB: Uribe.

White Sox	IP	H	R	ER	BB	SO
Buehrle	7.0	7	4	4	0	6
Politte	1.0	0	0	0	0	1
Jenks (BS)	0.2	2	2	2	1	1
Cotts (W)	0.1	0	0	0	0	0
Totals	9.0	9	6	6	1	8

HBP: Dye (by Wheeler); T: 3:11 (:07 delay); Att: 41,432.

The White Sox mob Scott Podsednik at home plate after his walk-off home run won the game for the Sox.
Photo by Tom Cruze/Sun-Times

swing on this fastball.' It was a good pitch to hit, and I was able to drive it out."

Just a half-inning earlier, Podsednik could have ended it on a throw to the plate. The Sox had a 6-4 lead and closer Jenks on the mound. With Chris Burke on second and Jeff Bagwell on third with two outs, pinch hitter Luis Vizcaino hit a sharp single to left field.

Podsednik came up with the ball, seemed to hesitate and fired a weak throw just to the left of home plate. A.J. Pierzynski reached toward the plate just behind a sliding Burke.

The runs tied the score and prevented a seventh-inning grand slam by Konerko from supplying the game-winning margin.

Earlier in October, Konerko helped win the clincher in the Division Series with a home run off the Boston Red Sox' Tim Wakefield to give the Sox their go-ahead runs. He won the MVP of the American League Championship Series mostly because of two first-inning home runs in victories over the Los Angels Angeles. Who knew he was just warming up?

Paul Konerko tips his cap to Sox fans after hitting a grand slam in the seventh and putting the Sox up by two runs.
Photo by Jon Sall/Sun-Times

After he delivered at least 40 home runs in each of his last two seasons, the biggest long ball of his life came on the first pitch from reliever Chad Qualls to put the Sox up 6-4 and move them six outs from victory. It was the first grand slam in postseason history for the Sox.

"It's just one of those things that [a home run] is the last thing on your mind," Konerko said. "I'm thinking to get a base hit to drive in two and hopefully tie and bang, you get it. That's usually when you get them is when you're not trying to. I didn't want to get in a long at-bat with him because I didn't feel that great tonight."

Two more victories remain for the Sox to partake in their fourth champagne party since Sept. 29, and this one surely would top all the others.

Mark Buehrle handled the duties in Game 2 and kept the Sox in the game long enough for a rally. After the Sox fell behind 1-0 in the second on a home run from Morgan Ensberg, they responded by getting the kind of breaks that have typified a run to a championship.

The Sox scored one of their two second-inning runs when veteran Craig Biggio dropped a pop-up in short right field.

"Clearly, everything they're doing right now is right," Astros manager Phil Garner said. "They can't do anything wrong. And so a lot of things are going their way. Even if they check swing and break a bat, they move a runner along."

After the second inning, the dean of postseason pitching managed to get the Sox out of their rhythm. Andy Pettitte made his 34th career playoff start Sunday, the most of anyone in postseason history. He allowed just two runs on eight hits in six innings.

Pettitte's departure after six innings was just what the Sox needed, although another break just before Konerko's home run proved to be huge. Dye loaded the bases in the seventh when home-plate umpire Jeff Nelson ruled Dye was hit by a pitch. Television replays showed that the ball actually hit Dye's bat.

Starter Mark Buehrle pitches in the second inning. Buehrle struck out six Astros in the game. Photo by John J. Kim/Sun-Times

Konerko, who entered with franchise highs of four homers and 11 RBIs in the postseason, added to the totals when his grand slam landed in the aisle to the center-field side of the Sox' bullpen, sending the crowd of 41,432 into a frenzy.

"You follow the team year-round, that's the way we play all year," manager Ozzie Guillen said.

"We keep fighting, making a big pitch. When somebody fails, pick [him] up. I went to take Jenks out, and A.J. is behind me and said, 'We'll come back, don't worry about it.' That's the attitude I like to hear. That's because of the unity they have."

—Written by Doug Padilla

WORLD SERIES GAME-ENDING HOMERS

Player's team listed first, with year, game, inning and final score:

Scott Podsednik: White Sox vs. Houston, 2005, Game 2, 9th, 7-6

Alex Gonzalez: Florida vs. N.Y. Yankees, 2003, Game 4, 12th, 4-3

Derek Jeter: N.Y. Yankees vs. Arizona, 2001, Game 4, 10th, 4-3

Chad Curtis: N.Y. Yankees vs. Atlanta, 1999, Game 3, 10th, 6-5

x-Joe Carter: Toronto vs. Philadelphia, 1993, Game 6, 9th, 8-6

Kirby Puckett: Minnesota vs. Atlanta, 1991, Game 6, 11th, 4-3

Mark McGwire: Oakland vs. Los Angeles, 1988, Game 3, 9th, 2-1

Kirk Gibson: Los Angeles vs. Oakland, 1988, Game 1, 9th, 5-4

Carlton Fisk: Boston vs. Cincinnati, 1975, Game 6, 12th, 7-6

Mickey Mantle: N.Y. Yankees vs. St. Louis, 1964, Game 3, 9th, 2-1

x-Bill Mazeroski: Pittsburgh vs. N.Y. Yankees, 1960, Game 7, 9th, 10-9

Eddie Mathews: Milwaukee vs. N.Y. Yankees, 1957, Game 4, 10th, 7-5

Dusty Rhodes: N.Y. Giants vs. Cleveland, 1954, Game 1, 10th, 5-2

Tommy Henrich: N.Y. Yankees vs. Brooklyn, 1949, Game 1, 9th, 1-0

x-clinched Series

Scott Podsednik hits a walk-off home run off Astros' pitcher Brad Lidge. Photo by Jon Sall/Sun-Times

SOXPULLOUTABLUM

WHITE SOX 7, ASTROS 5
OCTOBER 25, 2005
MINUTE MAID PARK

	1	2	3	4	5	6	7	8	9	10	11	12	13	14	R	H	E
White Sox	0	0	0	0	5	0	0	0	0	0	0	0	0	2	7	14	3
Astros	1	0	2	1	0	0	0	1	0	0	0	0	0	0	5	8	1

White Sox	AB	R	H	RBI	BB	SO
Podsednik, LF	8	1	2	0	0	2
Iguchi, 2B	7	1	2	1	0	1
Marte, P	0	0	0	0	0	0
Buehle, P	0	0	0	0	0	0
Dye, RF	7	1	2	1	0	1
Konerko, 1B	4	0	1	0	2	0
Pierzynski, C	3	0	1	2	2	0
Hernandez, P	0	0	0	0	0	0
Vizcaino, P	0	0	0	0	0	0
b-Perez, PH	1	0	0	0	0	0
Jenks, P	0	0	0	0	0	0
Blum, 2B	1	1	1	1	0	0
Rowand, CF	6	1	1	0	1	3
Crede, 3B	5	1	2	1	1	0
Uribe, SS	6	1	1	0	1	1
Garland, P	3	0	0	0	0	2
a-Everett, PH	1	0	1	0	0	0
Harris, PR	0	0	0	0	0	0
Politte, P	0	0	0	0	0	0
Cotts, P	0	0	0	0	0	0
Hermanson, P	0	0	0	0	0	0
Widger, C	1	0	0	1	2	1
Totals	53	7	14	7	9	11

a-Singled for Garland in the 8th. b-Grounded out for Vizcaino in the 11th.
2B: Konerko, Pierzynski; HR: Crede, Blum; E: Uribe 2, Hernandez.

White Sox	IP	H	R	ER	BB	SO
Garland	7.0	7	4	2	2	4
Politte	0.2	0	1	1	1	1
Cotts	0.0	0	0	0	1	0
Hermanson (BS)	0.1	1	0	0	0	1
Hernandez	1.0	0	0	0	4	2
Vizcaino	1.0	0	0	0	1	0
Jenks	2.0	0	0	0	1	3
Marte (W)	1.2	0	0	0	2	3
Buehrle (S)	0.1	0	0	0	0	0
Totals	14.0	8	5	3	12	14

Astros	AB	R	H	RBI	BB	SO
Biggio, 2B	6	2	2	1	1	3
Astacio, P	0	0	0	0	0	0
Rodriguez, P	0	0	0	0	0	0
Taveras, CF	6	0	0	0	0	3
Berkman, LF-1B	5	0	2	1	2	1
Ensberg, 3B	6	1	1	1	1	3
Lamb, 1B	3	0	0	0	1	0
Bruntlett, PR-LF	0	0	0	0	0	0
Lidge, P	0	0	0	0	0	0
b-Palmeiro, PH-LF	1	0	0	0	2	0
Lane, RF	6	1	2	2	1	0
Ausmus, C	6	0	0	0	1	2
Everett, SS	5	1	1	0	1	1
Oswalt, P	1	0	0	0	0	0
Springer, P	0	0	0	0	0	0
a-Bagwell, PH	1	0	0	0	0	0
Wheeler, P	0	0	0	0	0	0
Gallo, P	0	0	0	0	0	0
Burke, LF	1	0	0	0	1	0
Qualls, P	0	0	0	0	0	0
c-Vizcaino, PH-2B	0	0	0	0	1	0
Totals	47	5	8	5	12	14

a-Popped out for Springer in the 7th. b-Walked for Lidge in the 10th. c-Walked for Qualls in the 13th.

2B: Biggio, Lane; HR: Lane; E: Ensberg.

Astros	IP	H	R	ER	BB	SO
Oswalt	6.0	8	5	5	5	3
Springer	1.0	0	0	0	0	1
Wheeler	1.1	1	0	0	0	0
Gallo	0.1	0	0	0	0	0
Lidge	1.1	0	0	0	0	3
Qualls	3.0	1	0	0	2	3
Astacio (L)	0.2	4	2	2	2	0
Rodriguez	0.1	0	0	0	0	1
Totals	14.0	14	7	7	9	11

HBP: Taveras (by Jenks), Crede (by Oswalt), Konerko (by Wheeler); T: 5:41; Att: 42,848.

Geoff Blum, a late-inning Sox substitute, connects for a tie-breaking, two-out, solo home run in the 14th. It proved to be the game-winner. Photo by Tom Cruze/Sun-Times

In a run that has been pure magic, the White Sox moved one victory away from making their 88-year championship drought disappear.

Geoff Blum, who was acquired at the trade deadline more for his versatility than his impact ability, made his mark with a home run in the 14th inning to help the Sox to a 7-5 victory over the Houston Astros and a 3-0 lead in the World Series. The solo shot with two outs was Blum's second since he was acquired from the San Diego Padres for minor-league pitcher Ryan Meaux.

"I didn't know if I got it high enough," Blum said. "Somebody was watching out for me."

The 5-hour, 41-minute game was the longest by time in World Series history and tied for the longest in innings.

After the Sox went through their entire bullpen, Game 2 starter Mark Buehrle recorded the final out with the tying run on first base. Buehrle induced a pop-up from Adam Everett for the final out.

If 14 innings isn't enough for the home team to beat you, it might just be time to start engraving the World Series trophy to recognize a Sox team that is about to complete one of the most convincing runs in postseason history.

The Sox won for the 10th time in 11 postseason games by dispatching what was supposed to have been their toughest test yet in Houston Astros' 20-game winner Roy Oswalt. A fifth-inning uprising did the trick as the Sox sent 11 batters to the plate and delivered five runs on six hits. The five runs

Jermaine Dye and Tadahito Iguchi celebrate after scoring on A.J. Pierzynski's double deep to centerfield and taking the lead from the Astros in the fifth inning. Photo by Tom Cruze/Sun-Times

matched Oswalt's total in three previous postseason starts.

The Astros were held to one hit after the fourth inning and stranded 15 runners. They left the potential winning run at third base in the ninth and at second base in the 10th and 11th.

"It's some pretty poor hitting," Astros manager Phil Garner said. "We had our chances; it's amazing we were in the ballgame.

"We didn't hit the ball good, but we managed to stay in the game. Very frustrated. This is embarrassing, the way it's playing out."

Joe Crede, who has been as big as anybody for the Sox in the playoffs, opened the fifth inning with a home run and closed it on first base after getting hit in the ribs by an Oswalt fastball.

Jon Garland was far from sharp in his first World Series start, but then again, no Sox starter has dominated in the Series.

After Crede's home run, his second of the World Series and third of the postseason, Juan Uribe singled. A single by Scott Podsednik put runners on first and second before Tadahito Iguchi singled to cut the Astros' lead to 4-2. Jermaine Dye followed with an RBI single as the deficit was reduced to a run with Paul Konerko coming to the plate. But the hottest Sox hitter flied out. No matter. A.J. Pierzynski, who was moved up to the No. 5 spot in the batting order since Carl Everett was on the bench, hit a two-run double, with the ball kicking off the wall and rolling onto the hill in center field.

Mark Buehrle, the scheduled starter for Game 4, hugs catcher Chris Widger after the Sox made the final out to end the game.
Photo by Jon Sall/Sun-Times

Garland gave up a leadoff double in the first inning to Craig Biggio and a one-out RBI single to Lance Berkman as the Astros went on top 1-0. In the third inning, Garland looked like his night would come to an early close.

Adam Everett had a leadoff single to bring Oswalt to the plate. Manager Ozzie Guillen elected to pitch out on the first pitch, and Everett was caught off first base. Pierzynski threw to Juan Uribe at second base and Uribe ran Everett back to first. But his throw to Konerko hit Everett and allowed him to get back to the bag safely.

Oswalt delivered the sacrifice and Biggio followed with an RBI single. After a single from Berkman, Morgan Ensberg drove in a run before

Garland got out of the mess by striking out Mike Lamb.

In the fourth, another call went against the Sox as Jason Lane crushed a ball to left-center field and was credited with a home run even though television replays seemed to show that the ball should have been in play. Lane's drive appeared to hit to the left of a stripe painted on the outfield wall when only balls hit to the right are considered home runs.

But Crede's home run, on an 0-1 pitch, was the spark the Sox needed. Even Garland seemed to get a lift from the rally, retiring nine of the last 10 batters he faced in seven innings of work. In the eighth, Garland gave way to Cliff Politte, who retired his first two batters before giving up a walk to Ensberg. Neal Cotts came on to make his third appearance in three World Series games and walked Lamb.

Dustin Hermanson was called on for his first appearance since Sept. 30 and gave up a game-tying double to Lane before getting Ausmus on a strikeout. Orlando Hernandez, Luis Vizcaino, Bobby Jenks and even Damaso Marte held down the Astros over the final six innings. Marte earned the victory with 1-2/3 scoreless innings before Buehrle came on.

—Written by Doug Padilla

SOX TAKE THE FIFTH

Here's a look at the White Sox' fifth inning. Houston led 4-0 after four behind Roy Oswalt, who threw a career-high 46 pitches in the inning:

Joe Crede: Home run to right; 4-1.
Juan Uribe: Single to left.
Jon Garland: Strike out swinging.
Scott Podsednik: Single to right, first and second.
Tadahito Iguchi: RBI single to center, scores Uribe, first and second; 4-2.
Jermaine Dye: RBI single to center, scores Podsednik, first and second; 4-3.
Paul Konerko: Fly out to center.
A.J. Pierzynski: Two-run double to center, scores Iguchi and Dye; 5-4.
Aaron Rowand: Walk.
Crede: Hit by pitch, bases loaded.
Uribe: Fly out to center.

TOTALS: Five runs, six hits, no errors, three LOB.

Geoff Blum and the White Sox celebrate after beating the Astros, 7-5, in Game 3 of the World Series. Photo by Jon Sall/Sun-Times

BELIEVE IT!

WHITE SOX 1, ASTROS 0
OCTOBER 26, 2005
MINUTE MAID PARK

The White Sox will bring a championship back to 35th Street for the first time in 88 years, and this one will be a worldly affair.

The four-game World Series sweep was not just toasted on the South Side, it was celebrated in Tokyo, Caracas and Havana. There was reason for hugs and handshakes in the Dominican Republic, home to five Sox players. Even the Netherlands can

feel good about this one because trainer Herm Schneider was born there and is a veteran of 26 previous seasons, all void of titles.

Venezuela's Freddy Garcia reached down and showed just why he's considered a big-game pitcher as he paced the 1-0 victory over the Houston Astros with seven scoreless innings. His outing could've been dedicated to all the great Sox pitch-

	1	2	3	4	5	6	7	8	9	R	H	E
White Sox	0	0	0	0	0	0	0	1	0	1	8	0
Astros	0	0	0	0	0	0	0	0	0	0	5	0

White Sox	AB	R	H	RBI	BB	SO
Podsednik, LF	3	0	1	0	0	0
Iguchi, 2B	3	0	0	0	0	0
a-Everett, PH	1	0	0	0	0	0
Politte, P	0	0	0	0	0	0
Cotts, P	0	0	0	0	0	0
Jenks, P	0	0	0	0	0	0
Dye, RF	4	0	3	1	0	1
Konerko, 1B	4	0	0	0	0	2
Pierzynski, C	4	0	1	0	0	1
Rowand, CF	4	0	1	0	0	2
Crede, 3B	4	0	1	0	0	2
Uribe, SS	4	0	0	0	0	2
Garcia, P	2	0	0	0	0	0
b-Harris, PH-2B	1	1	1	0	0	0
Totals	34	1	8	1	0	10

a-Grounded to second for Iguchi in the 8th. b-Singled to left for Garcia in the 8th.

2B: Dye, Crede, Pierzynski; 3B: Podsednik.

White Sox	IP	H	R	ER	BB	SO
Garcia (W)	7.0	4	0	0	3	7
Politte	0.2	0	0	0	1	0
Cotts	0.1	0	0	0	0	0
Jenks (S)	1.0	1	0	0	0	0
Totals	9.0	5	0	0	4	7

Astros	AB	R	H	RBI	BB	SO
Biggio, 2B	4	0	1	0	0	0
Taveras, CF	2	0	1	0	0	0
Berkman, LF-1B	1	0	0	0	3	1
Ensberg, 3B	4	0	0	0	0	2
Lamb, 1B	2	0	1	0	1	0
b-Vizcaino, PH-1B	1	0	0	0	0	0
Lane, RF	4	0	1	0	0	2
Ausmus, C	3	0	1	0	0	1
Everett, SS	3	0	0	0	0	0
c-Burke, PH	1	0	0	0	0	0
Backe, P	2	0	0	0	0	1
a-Bagwell, PH	1	0	0	0	0	0
Lidge, P	0	0	0	0	0	0
d-Palmeiro, PH	1	0	0	0	0	0
Totals	29	0	5	0	4	7

a-Grounded to second for Backe in the 7th. b-Grounded to shortstop for Lamb in the 8th. c-Fouled out to shortstop for Everett in the 9th. d-Grounded to shortstop for Lidge in the 9th.

2B: Lamb; SB: Berkman, Taveras.

Astros	IP	H	R	ER	BB	SO
Backe	7.0	5	0	0	0	7
Lidge (L)	2.0	3	1	1	0	3
Totals	9.0	8	1	1	0	10

HBP: Taveras (by Politte); Time: 3:20; Attendance: 42,936

Jerry Reinsdorf and the White Sox celebrate after sweeping the Astros in the World Series.
Photo by Jon Sall/Sun-Times

ers who never finished a season on top with the club.

Ted Lyons. Billy Pierce. Hoyt Wilhelm. Wilbur Wood. Gary Peters. Jack McDowell. Bobby Thigpen. LaMarr Hoyt. Roberto Hernandez. Jim Kaat.

As far as the Astros are concerned, Sacramento, Calif., native Jermaine Dye is one of the toughest outs in baseball. His third hit of the game was a two-out, eighth-inning single up the middle to score Willie Harris and wrap up the World Series MVP. Dye's clutch performance helped the Sox raise the World Series trophy in the

locker room afterward, something that many of the great hitters in franchise history never did in Chicago.

Dick Allen. Luis Aparicio. Luke Appling. Chico Carrasquel. Carlton Fisk. Nellie Fox. Jim Landis. Sherm Lollar. Bill Melton. Minnie Minoso. Robin Ventura.

And it was all tied together by another Venezuelan in manager Ozzie Guillen, who went from third-base coach of the champion Florida Marlins in 2003 to winning manager of the Sox in 2005. He has been credited with supplying the glue that has kept one of the most cohesive teams

Pinch runner Willie Harris scores the only run of the game as Jermaine Dye races to first base with an RBI single.
Photo by Tom Cruze/Sun-Times

in baseball together from Day One. He ended up taking the Sox where many other team managers failed to go.

Jimmy Dykes. Al Lopez. Tony La Russa. Jerry Manuel. Paul Richards. Chuck Tanner. Kid Gleason. Gene Lamont. Jeff Torborg.

"You know what, we were just trying to win 11 games," A.J. Pierzynski said. "We went 11-1 in the playoffs and won every game on the road, and that's what we did all year. It was only fitting it ended up 1-0. That's the way we started the year [on Opening Day], that's the way we started the second half and that's the way it should have ended."

Guillen had the left-handed-hitting Harris pinch-hit for Garcia to open the eighth against Astros right-hander Brad Lidge. He could've chosen Game 3 hero Geoff Blum, a switch hitter, to take the assignment, but Harris stepped in and hit a single the opposite way to left field.

Scott Podsednik, who won Game 2 with a home run, came through this time by laying down

a bunt to move Harris to second. A ground ball by pinch hitter Carl Everett moved Harris to third to let Dye take over the hero's role for a day against Lidge.

"I had a game plan going up there," Dye said of the game-winning at-bat. "I know he throws a lot of sliders. He throws hard, but usually his fastball is just to keep you honest.

"I just stayed with my game plan, didn't try to do too much, just tried to hit it hard somewhere and found a hole up the middle."

The eighth inning nearly proved costly as Cliff Politte put runners on first and third with two outs before he was replaced by left-hander Neal Cotts.

Jose Vizcaino, who tied Game 2 in the ninth inning, connected on a broken-bat slow roller to shortstop that Juan Uribe backhanded and threw to first in time to leave the Sox three outs away.

Rookie closer Bobby Jenks entered in the ninth, and with the help of more Uribe defense, he closed out the game. Jenks gave up a leadoff single, was given an out on a sacrifice bunt by Brad Ausmus and Uribe took over. First he chased a foul pop-up down the left-field line, making the catch on the run while reaching into the crowd.

On the final out, Uribe charged a slow bouncer over the mound by Orlando Palmeiro, fielded it on the run and threw to Paul Konerko at first base to record the out by less than a half-step.

"Pitching and defense have been our thing all year long, and we stuck with our game plan," said Joe Crede, who would've been a worthy series MVP himself. "Defense is such a huge part of this game, and the second you relax out there and make an error, it seems like they capitalize on it."

After both offenses struggled late into the night in Game 3, they continued with that theme in Game 4.

Garcia, who picked up the victory in both the Central Division clincher and the Division Series clincher, held back an offense that had been ripped by its own manager one night earlier.

After the Sox won Game 3 in the 14th inning, an angry Phil Garner questioned his team's approach at the plate.

The Astros didn't score over the final 19 innings of the series.

"Let me say this, I congratulate the Chicago White Sox," Garner said. "They had a phenomenal year. My hat's off to them. They played well all year long, and in the playoffs, they played well and they played well against us.

"They deserve to be called world champions this year, but our team is a winner, too."

Just as in the ALDS and the ALCS, there was just too much clutch hitting from the Sox.

"Hopefully, a lot of people were partying, and they didn't get too rowdy or in too much trouble," Pierzynski said.

"But at the same time, I hope they lived it up and partied like it's 1917."

—Written by Doug Padilla

After making an impossible throw to Paul Konerko at first base for the final out of the game, Juan Uribe and Konerko embrace in the infield. Photo by Tom Cruze/Sun-Times

The World Champion Chicago White Sox storm the field after the final out was made in Minute Maid Park.

Photo by Tom Cruze/Sun-Times

AFTER 88 YEARS OF FRUSTRATION, SOX FANS CHEER FOR THEIR CHAMPIONS

Eighty-eight years of futility? Roll over Shoeless Joe and tell Kid Gleason the news: It's done. For the first time in a lifetime, the words Chicago and White Sox and World Champions can be spoken in the same breath. Make that screamed. Hollered. Howled. Shrieks of joy, sure, but more than that. Catharsis. With the White Sox' victory over Houston, the heartbreaks and black eyes of the past can fade into their proper perspective. The 1919 Black Sox scandal, the 1959 close-but-no-cigar, the '67 stumble, Disco Demolition, uniforms with shorts, the Florida Sox and Father-Son Beatdown Night are now just footnotes, not enduring tales of woe. "Win or die trying" was the team motto. Long live the White Sox.

Scott Podsednik described this year's White Sox as "25 guys pulling on the same rope." True enough—but the speedy left fielder was a few million short on the count. Fans, too, were pulling for the team, of course. And they were pulling for friends and family—some who left this Earth without ever hearing the words World Champion and White Sox in the same breath. They pulled for the buddies with whom they had their first beer (a Falstaff?) at Comiskey Park, or the date they split the churro with, or maybe the Old Man who taught them that a double play is 6-4-3 on the scorecard. But they were also pulling for themselves. Sports divert us from the routines of life—the drudgeries of the 49th floor cubicle of the Sears Tower and the miseries of navigating the Ike. A double off the wall offers a coherence and clarity in a complicated 1040-form world.

A TEAM OF THE EVERYMAN

Sports also offer us heroes to emulate—and with the White Sox, there was a smorgasbord to select from: a black general manager, a Hispanic field manager, a home run-hitting Caucasian, an Asian second sacker. And this was a team of the everyman: Few fans as kids were star pitchers, a la Jon Garland. Most of us were more like Geoff Blum, the benchwarmer who settled a 14-inning contest Tuesday with an unlikely shot to the right field seats. Or like portly pitcher Bobby Jenks.

A.J. Pierzynski was born in Bridgehampton, N.Y., but the catcher's cockiness was pure Bridgeport, Chicago.

Phil Arrendondo, 41, a pipefitter watching the game at T's Tap, 9801 S. Ewing, identified with third baseman Joe Crede, calling him a "steamship" because "he starts it and every one else follows."

At the United Center, Joe Park, 36, from Hinsdale, a beauty supply store owner, praised the play of first baseman Paul Konerko.

"He's even-keeled, he's mild-mannered, he's a hard-working guy. That's what Chicago's all about."

Guillen for mayor? That fans see themselves in their athletes is not uncommon, said Michael Mandelbaum, author of *The Meaning of Sports*. And that connection then extends to their fellow fans.

"As people identify with the team, they're also identifying with each other," said Mandelbaum. "So, when a team wins, everyone feels a part of the same community."

In Chicago, not quite the same community. With hard-held allegiances split between the Sox and Cubs, the World Series victory was not quite the same kind of local lovefest fostered by the Michael Jordan-led Bulls or the 1985 Bears. But the championship certainly galvanized the Sox supporters.

"The Sox have been the stepchild for all these years. The Cubs have been the glamorous rich guy who gets the girl. And suddenly the White Sox have been elected class president," said Mandelbaum.

(They might just elect manager Ozzie Guillen something else. Riding a wave of popularity, the straight-talking former Sox player joked on national TV, "Watch out Mayor Daley, I'm going for you!")

Baseball is best as a shared experience. And so fans gathered in houses, they crowded into bars and hunkered down in restaurants to watch their team capture the crown.

FAMILY TRADITION

As the Sox won a 1-0 squeaker, fans roared into the streets, including around U.S. Cellular Field, where they were met by watchful police. While in 1959, the city shook up some by sounding the air raid sirens, this time the sounds of joy were punctuated with another disturbing noise: gunfire. Some set Astros hats afire. Outside Puffer's on Halsted in Bridgeport, Jose Maestre was thinking not only of his father but his grandfather and grandmother, too—the lineage that gave him his White Sox identity.

"Even though they're not here anymore, I'm here for them," said Maestre, a 46-year-old mover from Uptown.

'BEAUTIFUL MEMORIES'

In the front yard of the site where they grew up, near 35th and Lowe, the five children of Rita and Patrick McGuinness set up a TV, warmed themselves around a small firepit and talked of how, in the words of one daughter, "none of us would be here if it wasn't for the White Sox."

Rita and Patrick, now deceased, had their first date at Comiskey Park in 1949. The game went into extra innings and Patrick, recently arrived from Ireland, had no idea of what was happening on the field. But he did know he liked Rita. The children grew up listening to the games on the radio on the back porch or on TV—the mother taught them to encourage the players through the screen, "and we still do it," said Noreen McGuinness, 40ish.

The Sox lost games "all our lives" but "we still went because we like the game," said Theresa McGuinness, 48. The national television ratings suggested that the country was yawning.

But in these parts, the World Series was as if a new holiday had suddenly been invented—a new kind of Christmas week where work and school were lightened by talk of bunts and beanballs. For 95-year-old Lowell Frasor, this year's White Sox season is the latest addition in his collection of "beautiful memories"—memories of hearing his dad talk about the 1917 World Series (Frasor was 7), seeing "Shoeless" Joe Jackson play at Old Comiskey in 1919 (bleacher seats were 50 cents) and attending the first game of the 1959 World Series.

AROUND FOR BOTH TITLES

A retired bank exec from Blue Island, now a resident at the Washington and Jane Smith retirement community in the Beverly neighborhood, listens to every game on the radio. But even approaching 100, Frasor was amazed that he would experience another White Sox championship, much less a sweep.

"It's actually something I never expected," said Frasor.

He could have been speaking for a stunned but delighted White Sox nation.

—Written by Andrew Herrmann

MVP JERMAINE DYE

Roster of MVPs Produced Memorable Season

By Chris De Luca

White Sox right fielder Jermaine Dye deserved to be the World Series MVP as much as anyone.

You could make a case for third baseman Joe Crede.

You could even form an argument for first baseman Paul Konerko.

Don't forget pitcher Mark Buehrle.

And didn't infielder Geoff Blum and catcher A.J. Pierzynski do some nice things during a World Series sweep of the Houston Astros that now seems like a blur?

"Stars? We've got stars," Pierzynski said, dousing Crede with champagne. "We've got Crede."

Fact is, anyone could have been pulled out of the Sox' clubhouse and given the MVP Award. And that's the thing about the 2005 White Sox. Someone different stepped up every day, from the moment they moved into first place with a 1-0 victory against the Cleveland Indians on Opening Day until they wrapped up the World Series with another 1-0 victory.

Dye had impressive credentials during the 101st World Series. He hit .438 (7-for-16) with one home run and three RBI during the four games. His two-out single in the eighth inning provided all the scoring a Sox team built around pitching would need.

"When you've got a lot of guys that can get

Dye, who was making his second World Series appearance after a trip to the 1996 Series as a rookie with the Atlanta Braves. "A couple of guys could have got it. We all worked hard to do whatever we could to help this team win and guys came up with big hits in a lot of situations. And it's just special for me to be thought of as MVP and become an MVP in that group."

Dye came through against Astros closer Brad Lidge in the eighth.

Pinch hitter Willie Harris led off the inning with a single. Two outs later, Harris was on third and the Sox knew they were on the brink of a breakthrough.

Dye stepped to the plate full of confidence.

"I had a game plan going up there," he said. "I know he throws a lot of sliders. He throws hard but usually his fastball is just to keep you honest. And I stuck with the game plan of going up there, looking for a slider and just not trying to do too much with it. The first pitch he threw me was a slider. I swung kind of too hard and then threw me another one for a ball, and I stayed with my game plan, didn't really try to do too much, just tried to hit it hard somewhere and found a hole up the middle."

Another clutch hit, another Sox hero.

"It's a true team," said injured slugger Frank Thomas, who used to bat in Dye's No. 3 spot. "It doesn't matter who got you. [Geoff] Blum came off the bench [in Game 3] and got you. Willie Harris came off the bench and got you tonight. It's about team. These guys cared about each other. It's a special moment for this team. These guys deserved

Crede came of age during this postseason.

After the kind of solid, but not spectacular, season manager Ozzie Guillen said we should expect from Crede, the third baseman came alive in the postseason, proving to be a consistently clutch player.

"This has definitely helped my confidence," Crede said. "Baseball is all about having a lot of confidence. Playing in the clutch, there is not a bigger series to play in than the World Series. And if you can perform at the highest level, it's a great feeling."

It was a dominating postseason run by the Sox, who went 11-1—losing only Game 1 of the American League Championship Series.

Did general manager Ken Williams envision such dominance in the postseason?

"No," he said. "That was impressive and humbling at the same time. The pride I feel for playing for this particular group ... a lot of people don't know because they just see them in uniform, but these are good guys. Guys that you will make lifelong friends with. These are the kinds of guys that you want—well, not all of them, but some of them—your daughter to marry."

This joyride of a season ended abruptly.

But there will be no more baseball for the Sox in 2005.

Hard to imagine.

"I don't want to play anymore baseball this year, I know that," Crede said.

"We counted them up the other day and we've played over 200 baseball games this year. These games are not only physically draining, they are mentally draining. I just want to sit back and enjoy this, relish it and soak it all up while it's here."

SPECIAL SEASON CHANGES EVERYTHING

Just like that, with a tumble and a toss by Juan Uribe, as if 88 years never passed, so ended a city's blind spot, its black hole, its burden of time, an agonizing void that created an inferiority complex in a place inferior to none. What Chicago ever did to suffer almost a century of baseball hopelessness, you'll have to ask the evil spirits or Mrs. O'Leary's cow. But finally, America's most unfulfilled baseball town has the same prize as Boston and, um, Phoenix and Miami.

That would be a 30-pound trophy, made of brass and pewter, with pretty flags.

Behold the city's most special baseball season of our time—of all time, really. Wrap yourself in glory that might not match the civic totality of the 1985 Bears and the Bulls dynasty, but certainly tops it in South Side precincts. Wednesday night, the White Sox won the friggin' World Series. Not only is this tantamount to sushi bars replacing deep-dish parlors, this also has legions of grown men crying, wishing their fathers and grandfathers could see what the impossible looks like.

One of those fighting tears was Jerry Reinsdorf, who stood in the Sox clubhouse with his longtime friend and partner in crime, Bud Selig, and accepted the trophy. Have I sparred with Reinsdorf through the years? Yes. Was I happy the man finally won? Yes.

"Twenty-five years ago, you got me into this game," he said to Selig on the podium. "And most of those of those 25 years, I asked you why. I'll never ask you again.

"This is for all the fans in Chicago—South Side, North Side, West Side. I hope it's not a dream when I wake up in the morning."

Morning has broken. The headlines say the Sox swept the Houston Astros.

IT MATTERS HERE

A nation didn't watch. Hollywood won't script it. Cubdom is cringing, and the only poet who might wax is Jimbo, behind his bar on 33rd Street. But who really cares what the rest of the world thinks? A town known for its terminal baseball woe has been healed. And the team that broke through wasn't the bloated Cubs, the romanticized franchise with the well-moneyed fans and conglomerate ownership, but the maligned, forgotten team from the other side of town. Or should I now say the cool side of town, a side that reminded us where heart, passion, and grit reside? No longer must any of us dwell on the 1919 Black Sox, Disco Demolition Night, elephants, midgets, drunks on the field and decades of futility and identity crises. All of that was purged during a season-long plundering so convincing, from the chill of April to the hush of a Texas ballpark in late autumn, that it's tempting to say the 88-year wait was worth it.

"That was the first time in my life that my heart was pounding like crazy. I'm just happy for Jerry and the fans, because they've been waiting so long," said Ozzie Guillen, the one Sox manager who thrived when so many others failed. "This was my dream, my goal to win for this team."

So, are you coming back?

"Now I'm going to make my money," the Blizzard said. "We'll see what happens."

"Do I need a new manager or not?" shot back Ken Williams, the one Sox general manager who thrived when so many others failed.

Give Guillen a bonus, and he'll be back. He couldn't live without the fun, the buzz. In fact, the Sox were so much fun, even Cubs fans should acknowledge the brilliant feat and share a toast. Could this be a monumental moment in the blood war, a truce that would be healthy for the city's psyche after so much angst and socioeconomic-related rancor?

Is it still a Cubs town? Sure, it is, based on sheer numbers. Higher percentages of people watched the Series games in Houston than in Chicago, telling me a good share of Cubbie TVs weren't on. And when pressed, several Sox players said it's still a Cubs town, Paul Konerko and Aaron Rowand included. But here's the thing: They said it devilishly, with pride, thrilled to slay the beast.

Unlike the Cubs, the Sox didn't choke. They smoked, oozing of Ozzie and melding before our eyes in Williams's test tube. There was so much charm and symmetry for so many months, they almost seemed too good to be true, especially during a September free fall that had us all thinking the worst. Turns out the Sox were only teasing us with their slump. It toughened them mentally, allowed them to take a deep breath and empowered them to take on postseason opponents that looked better but ultimately weren't close to their caliber.

THE SECRET WAS SIMPLE

"People are looking for big theories. We've just got 25 hard-working, grind-it-out guys," Williams said. "We asked them one thing: Each and every one of them to leave it all out on the field. They did that more than any team I've ever seen. And Ozzie, the one thing we had in common was we wanted to see Bud Selig hand the trophy to Jerry."

A Chicago team, I've always said, finally will win it all when we least expect it. We expected the Cubs to win in 2003 because they had the requisite big names. But they collapsed when the heat was on, as opposed to the Sox, who recovered and conquered October like few teams in baseball history. Their 11-1 postseason record matches the 1999 Yankees' as the best record in the division-series era and ranks in the modern era behind only the

1976 Big Red Machine, which went 7-0. Dating back to those nervous nights in Detroit, one full month ago, the Sox lost one game.

Once.

What they did, thanks to the feisty leadership of Guillen and foresight of Williams, was write a new blueprint on how baseball might be played in the post-steroids era. They wanted selfless players and didn't care where they came from—America, Japan, Venezuela, Cuba, Puerto Rico. With everyone obeying and respecting the yakkety Guillen like some cult figure, the overhaul worked like few we've seen.

There was one star, Paul Konerko, and a Mount Soxmore rotation. Otherwise, solid players fulfilled roles splendidly and played smallball, bigball, whatever was needed—but always smartball. If you had told me Jermaine Dye, Magglio Ordonez's marginally received replacement, would be Series MVP, I'd have giggled loudly.

"A lot of guys on this team could have this award," Dye said.

The only regret is that the Sox never celebrated on the South Side. Detroit ... Boston ... Anaheim ... Houston ... road bashes, all. But thousands of fans still came. And deep in the night, they started a chant in the stands as the Sox party raged on the field.

"Bring that trophy over here!"

Naturally, someone did. The Sox never failed to deliver.

—Written by Jay Mariotti

2005 REGULAR SEASON STATISTICS

HITTING

Player	G	AB	R	H	2B	3B	HR	RBI	TB	BB	SO	SB	CS	OBP	SLG	AVG
Rowand	157	578	77	156	30	5	13	69	235	32	116	16	5	.329	.407	.270
Konerko	158	575	98	163	24	0	40	100	307	81	109	0	0	.375	.534	.283
Dye	145	529	74	145	29	2	31	86	271	39	99	11	4	.333	.512	.274
Iguchi	135	511	74	142	25	6	15	71	224	47	114	15	5	.342	.438	.278
Podsednik	129	507	80	147	28	1	0	25	177	47	75	59	23	.351	.349	.290
Everett	135	490	58	123	17	2	23	87	213	42	99	4	5	.311	.435	.251
Uribe	146	481	58	121	23	3	16	71	198	34	77	4	6	.301	.412	.252
Pierzynski	128	460	61	118	21	0	18	56	193	23	68	0	2	.308	.420	.257
Crede	132	432	54	109	21	0	22	62	196	25	66	1	1	.313	.330	.252
Ozuna	70	203	27	56	7	2	0	11	67	7	26	14	7	.313	.330	.276
Perez	76	179	13	39	8	0	2	15	53	12	25	2	2	.266	.296	.218
Widger	45	141	18	34	8	0	4	11	54	10	22	0	2	.296	.383	.241
Harris	56	121	17	31	2	1	1	8	38	13	25	10	3	.333	.314	.256
Thomas	34	105	19	23	3	0	12	26	62	16	31	0	0	.315	.590	.219
Blum	31	95	6	19	2	1	1	3	26	4	15	0	1	.232	.274	.200
Gload	28	42	2	7	2	0	0	5	9	2	9	0	0	.205	.214	.167
Anderson	13	34	3	6	1	0	2	3	13	0	12	1	0	.176	.382	.176
Borchard	7	12	0	5	2	0	0	0	7	0	4	0	1	.417	.583	.417
Garcia	3	7	0	0	0	0	0	0	0	0	1	0	0	.000	.000	.000
Lopez	2	7	1	2	0	0	0	2	2	0	1	0	0	.286	.286	.286
Casanova	6	5	0	1	0	0	0	0	1	0	1	0	0	.200	.200	.200
Buehrle	1	3	0	0	0	0	0	0	0	0	1	0	0	.000	.000	.000
Contreras	2	3	0	0	0	0	0	0	0	1	2	0	0	.250	.000	.000
Hernandez	1	3	0	1	0	0	0	0	1	0	1	0	0	.333	.333	.333
Garland	1	2	0	1	0	0	0	1	1	0	1	0	0	.500	.500	.500
McCarthy	1	2	0	0	0	0	0	0	0	0	2	0	0	.000	.000	.000
Burke	1	1	0	0	0	0	0	0	0	0	0	0	0	.000	.000	.000
Politte	5	1	1	1	0	0	0	1	1	0	0	0	0	1.000	1.000	1.000

PITCHING

Player	W	L	ERA	G	SV	IP	H	R	ER	BB	SO
Buehrle	16	8	3.12	33	0	236.2	240	99	82	40	149
Garcia	14	8	3.87	33	0	228.0	225	102	98	60	146
Garland	18	10	3.50	32	0	221.0	212	93	86	47	115
Contreras	15	7	3.61	32	0	204.2	177	91	82	75	154
Hernandez	9	9	5.12	24	1	128.1	137	77	73	50	91
Vizcaino	6	5	3.73	65	0	70.0	74	30	29	29	43
Politte	7	1	2.00	68	1	67.1	42	15	15	21	57
McCarthy	3	2	4.03	12	0	67.0	62	30	30	17	48
Cotts	4	0	1.94	69	0	60.1	38	15	13	29	58
Hermanson	2	4	2.04	57	34	57.1	46	17	13	17	33
Marte	3	4	3.77	66	4	45.1	45	21	19	33	54
Jenks	1	1	2.75	32	6	39.1	34	15	12	15	50
Takatsu	1	2	5.97	31	8	28.2	30	19	19	16	32
Adkins	0	1	8.64	5	0	8.1	13	8	8	4	1
Walker	0	1	9.00	9	0	7.0	10	7	7	5	5
Bajenaru	0	0	6.23	4	0	4.1	4	3	3	0	3
Sanders	0	0	13.50	2	0	2.0	3	3	3	1	1

NEWSPAPER CREDITS

We gratefully acknowledge the efforts of the *Chicago Sun-Times* photography department, which contributed to the coverage of the Chicago White Sox 2005 season, culminating in a World Series victory.

Nancy Stuenkel—Photography Director
Ernie Torres—Photo Assignment Editor
Dom Najolia—Photo Assignment Editor
Bob Black
Richard A. Chapman
Tom Cruze
Jim Frost
Keith Hale
Rich Hein
Brian Jackson
John J. Kim
Jean Lachat
Al Podgorski
Jon Sall
Scott Stewart
John H. White